Debating Points

Debating Points:
Contemporary Social Issues Series

Henry L. Tischler, Series Editor

Debating Points: Marriage and Family Issues
Henry L. Tischler
Debating Points: Race and Ethnic Relations
Henry L. Tischler

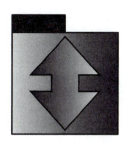

Debating Points:
Marriage and Family Issues

Henry L. Tischler, Editor

Framingham State College

Prentice
Hall

Upper Saddle River, New Jersey 07458

Library of Congress Cataloging-in-Publication Data

Debating points: marriage and family issues/[edited by] Henry L. Tischler.
   p. cm.—(Debating points—contemporary social issues)
  Includes bibliographical references.
  ISBN 0-13-799727-2
  1. Marriage—United States. 2. Family—United States. 3. United States—Social
conditions—1980–. I. Tischler, Henry L. II. Series.

  HQ536.D354 2000
  306.8'0973—dc21   00-055077

VP, Editorial director: Laura Pearson
Managing editor: Sharon Chambliss
Director of marketing: Beth Gillett Mejia
Editorial/production supervision: Kari Callaghan Mazzola
Prepress and manufacturing buyer: Mary Ann Gloriande
Electronic page makeup: Kari Callaghan Mazzola
Interior design: John P. Mazzola
Cover director: Jayne Conte
Cover design: Joe Sengotta

This book was set in 10/12 Meridien by Big Sky Composition
and was printed and bound by Courier Companies, Inc.
The cover was printed by Phoenix Color Corp.

© 2001 by Prentice-Hall, Inc.
A Division of Pearson Education
Upper Saddle River, New Jersey 07458

Printed in the United States of America
10 9 8 7 6 5 4 3 2

ISBN 0-13-799727-2

PRENTICE-HALL INTERNATIONAL (UK) LIMITED, *London*
PRENTICE-HALL OF AUSTRALIA PTY. LIMITED, *Sydney*
PRENTICE-HALL CANADA INC., *Toronto*
PRENTICE-HALL HISPANOAMERICANA, S.A., *Mexico*
PRENTICE-HALL OF INDIA PRIVATE LIMITED, *New Delhi*
PRENTICE-HALL OF JAPAN, INC., *Tokyo*
PEARSON EDUCATION ASIA PTE. LTD., *Singapore*
EDITORA PRENTICE-HALL DO BRASIL, LTDA., *Rio de Janeiro*

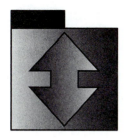

Contents

Preface

The *Debating Points: Contemporary Social Issues* series can be used to teach critical thinking, encourage student participation, and stimulate class discussion. Each book in this series is designed to provide readers with well-developed, carefully considered, and clearly written opposing viewpoints on a wide range of issues. A guiding principle in the selection of the issues for all *Debating Points* books is that they be easily understood and relevant to the backgrounds and interests of the students. Each issue within each book is self-contained and may be assigned according to the individual instructor's preferences or the dictates of classroom time.

The debate format used in each book in the *Debating Points* series helps students to understand the significance of the principles, concepts, and theories they are learning in class. It encourages students to apply critical thinking techniques to the opinions and statements that they see and hear around them. Students will see that some issues do not have "right" or "wrong" answers, and that it is important to grasp the different points of view in order to gain a fuller understanding of the issue. The purpose of the debate format is to stimulate interest in the subject matter and to encourage the application of concepts and ideas. The "yes" and "no" essays have been selected to reflect a variety of ideological viewpoints and have been edited to present the views in a concise and interesting manner. The authors of the essay selections have been chosen because they are creditable scholars or commentators who are respected in their fields.

In this second volume in the *Debating Points* series—*Debating Points: Marriage and Family Issues*—each issue begins with an introduction, which sets the stage for the debate by putting the issue into the context of a larger social science discussion and providing a brief description of the articles.

Each debate concludes with a list of websites that students can research for further information on the issue. The websites have been chosen to reflect the diversity of views presented in the readings. With the advent of new communication technologies and with growing awareness of the World Wide Web, students are being exposed more frequently to differing viewpoints and sometimes to questionable information. In order to process this information effectively, students are going to have to rely on their critical thinking skills. Combining the issue articles with corresponding websites allows students to continue to explore the issues for a fuller understanding.

Many instructors have recognized the importance of applying material that has been discussed in the classroom. The *Debating Points* series is an excellent tool for encouraging students to critically evaluate the utility of various theoretical perspectives. The push is on for educators to help students strengthen their critical thinking skills. The books in the *Debating Points* series are excellent tools for teaching critical thinking in that they expose students to a variety of viewpoints and to strongly argued positions related to their field of study.

Henry L. Tischler
Series Editor

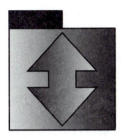

About the Contributors

JAMES Q. WILSON began his career as a professor of government at Harvard University in the 1960s, and has since earned a reputation as a criminologist, economist, and political analyst. He is the author or coauthor of 12 books, including *American Government*; *Thinking about Crime*; *Varieties of Police Behavior*; *Political Organizations*; *Crime and Human Nature*; *Bureaucracy*; and his most recent, *The Moral Sense*.

STEPHANIE COONTZ teaches history and family studies at The Evergreen State College in Olympia, Washington. She is the author of *The Way We Really Are: Coming to Terms with America's Changing Families* (1997) and *The Way We Never Were: American Families and the Nostalgia Trap* (1995). She is a former Woodrow Wilson fellow and received the Dale Richmond Award from the American Academy of Pediatrics for her "outstanding contributions to the field of child development" in 1995.

DAVID POPENOE is professor of sociology at Rutgers, the State University of New Jersey, where he also serves as social and behavioral sciences dean in the Faculty of Arts and Sciences. He is the author of several books, including *Disturbing the Nest: Family Change and Decline in Modern Society* (1988).

LOUISE B. SILVERSTEIN is an assistant professor of psychology at Yeshiva University. She is cofounder of the Yeshiva Fatherhood Project, a qualitative research study of fathering from a multicultural perspective. She is working on a book about the subjective experiences of fathers from 10 subcultures, including divorced, gay, Latino, and Modern Orthodox Jewish fathers.

CARL F. AUERBACH is acting director of Yeshiva University's Robert M. Beren Center for Psychological Intervention, which has established a national network of counselors interested in the dynamics of couples and families. His other interests are research methods, cognitive science, and psychotherapy.

MAGGIE GALLAGHER's opinion column has appeared in *Newsday* since 1993. Her articles have also appeared in *The New Republic*, the *Wall Street Journal, National Review,*

Cosmopolitan, and the *New York Times.* Gallagher is also the author of *Enemies of Eros: How the Sexual Revolution Is Killing Family, Marriage, and Sex* (1989) and of *The Abolition of Marriage* (1995). Currently she is an affiliate scholar at the Institute for American Values.

KRISTIN DROEGE is a research associate at the Milken Family Foundation.

WILLIAM A. GALSTON is a professor in the School of Public Affairs at the University of Maryland at College Park and director of the Institute for Philosophy and Public Policy. From 1993 to 1995 he was deputy assistant for domestic policy for President Clinton.

MARGARET TALBOT is a senior editor at *The New Republic* magazine.

LORI B. ANDREWS is a professor at Chicago-Kent College of Law and director of the Institute for Science, Law, and Technology. She is the author of 6 books and more than 80 articles on genetics, alternative modes of reproduction, and biotechnology. She has been an advisor on genetic and reproductive technology to the president and to Congress.

KAREN WRIGHT is a contributing editor at *Discover* magazine.

CATHY YOUNG is an associate policy analyst at the Cato Institute, a columnist with the *Detroit News,* and author of *Gender Wars* (in press).

DIANA ZUCKERMAN was a psychologist for several years before moving to Washington, D.C., to work for the House of Representatives and the Senate. She is a member of the National Coalition against Domestic Violence and of the Institute for Women's Policy Research.

ANDREW J. CHERLIN is Benjamin H. Griswold III Professor of Public Policy in the Department of Sociology at Johns Hopkins University. He studies the sociology of the family and social demography, with an emphasis on public policy issues such as the effects of family changes on the well-being of children. He is the author of *Public and Private Families: An Introduction* (1996) and *Marriage, Divorce, Remarriage* (1992), and coauthor of *Divided Families: What Happens to Children When Parents Part* with Frank F. Furstenberg Jr. (1991).

FRANK F. FURSTENBERG JR. is Zellerbach Family Professor of Sociology at the University of Pennsylvania and has published widely on the contemporary American family, including such topics as teenage childbearing and the effects of divorce. He is coauthor with Andrew J. Cherlin of *Divided Families: What Happens to Children When Parents Part* (1991).

VIRGINIA RUTTER is a professor at the University of Washington and coauthor with Pepper Schwartz of *The Gender of Sexuality: Exploring Sexual Possibilities* (1998).

ANDREW SULLIVAN worked as a summer intern at *The New Republic* during his student years. He later rose to editor in chief. Sullivan is the author of *Virtually Normal: An Argument about Homosexuality* (1995). He also edited a companion volume: *Same-Sex Marriage: Pro or Con, A Reader,* as well as *Love Undetectable: Notes on Friendship, Sex, and Survival.* Currently Sullivan writes a column on American politics for the *Sunday Times* of London.

Is the American Family in Trouble?

The traditional nuclear family, with the father as sole breadwinner and the mother staying home to raise the children, has become the exception rather than the rule. Higher levels of divorce and cohabitation, combined with lower marriage rates, have changed the structure of the American family. An increasingly common phenomenon is the female-headed household where the woman is the sole source of income and there is no adult male present.

Also, the size of the American household is declining. In the past 30 years the average household has gone from 3.1 to 2.6 people. One factor contributing to declining household size is that family life appears to be losing some of its appeal to young adults. More of them are choosing to postpone marriage, or not to get married at all. The percentage of adults living alone increased from 8 percent to 13 percent between 1970 and 1998. The percentage of the population that has never married increased from 22 percent to 28 percent in the past 30 years (*Population Today*, September 1999).

Parents are spending less time with their children and more time at work than ever. In 1996, 76.2 percent of married women with children between 6 and 17 worked outside the home. Nearly 63 percent of married women with children six and under did the same. Meanwhile, fathers of small children are not cutting back their hours at work to help out at home (*Statistical Abstract of the United States*, 1997). American men average 48.8 hours of work a week and women 41.7 hours, including overtime and commuting. All in all, more men and women are on an economic train that is running faster and faster.

There are several broader historical causes for these trends. The past 30 years have witnessed a rapid increase of women in the workplace. At the same time, job mobility has taken families farther from relatives who might lend a hand, and has made it harder to make close friends of neighbors who could help out. Moreover, as women have acquired more education and have joined men at work, they have absorbed the views of the male-oriented work world.

James Q. Wilson, in his essay "The Family Values Debate," states his belief that the American family has been in decline for the past few decades. He thinks that when people look at the dramatic increase in divorce, single-parent families, and illegitimate children that has taken place over the past 30 years, they see families in trouble. Wilson believes that people do not need studies to tell them that these are bad trends, because they have seen the consequences in their own lives or those of people they know. Divorce may sometimes be the right and necessary remedy for fundamentally flawed marriages and for the conditions created by an abusive or neglectful spouse, but in general divorce makes people worse off: The woman becomes poorer and the children become more distressed. Properly raising a child is an enormous responsibility that often taxes the efforts and energies of two parents; one parent is likely to be overwhelmed. Children born out of wedlock are, in the great majority of cases, children born into poverty, Wilson notes.

Stephanie Coontz, in her article "The American Family and the Nostalgia Trap," contends that criticizing the current American family structure poses serious dangers for people who sincerely want to improve the lives of their children. Of course values are important, she argues, but polarizing the issue as "their bad values versus our good ones" or "their bad parenting versus our commitment to kids" ignores the fact that all of us have bad values as well as good ones. It vastly underestimates the role of the external environment and of institutions in reinforcing some values while extinguishing others, and in letting some people get away with periodic lapses of personal responsibility while others pay dearly and permanently for even the smallest mistake. Beneath the seemingly sensible claim that the "breakdown of the family" causes all our social ills lies a simplistic analysis of how traditional family forms and gender roles used to operate, of where contemporary family problems originate, and of what parents can and should do to raise healthy children.

The Family Values Debate

James Q.
Wilson

There are two views about the contemporary American family, one held by the public and the other by policy elites.

...

The public's view is this: The family is the place in which the most basic values are instilled in children. In recent years, however, these values have become less secure, in part because the family has become weaker and in part because rivals for its influence—notably television and movies—have gotten stronger. One way the family has become weaker is that more and more children are being raised in one-parent families, and often that one parent is a teenage girl. Another way is that parents, whether in one- or two-parent families, are spending less time with their children and are providing poorer discipline. Because family values are so important, political candidates should talk about them, though it is not clear that the government can do much about them. Overwhelmingly, Americans think that it is better for children if one parent stays home and does not work, even if that means having less money.

No such consensus is found among scholars or policymakers. That in itself is revealing. Beliefs about families that most people regard as virtually self-evident are hotly disputed among people whose job it is to study or support families.

A good example of the elite argument began last fall on the front page of the *Washington Post*, where a reporter quoted certain social scientists as saying that the conventional two-parent family was not as important for the healthy development of children as was once supposed. This prompted

From *Commentary* 95, no. 1 (April 1993). Copyright © 1993. Reprinted with the permission of the author and *Commentary*.

David Popenoe, a professor at Rutgers who has written extensively on family issues, to publish in the *New York Times* an op-ed piece challenging the scholars cited in the *Post*. Popenoe asserted that "dozens" of studies had come to the opposite conclusion, and that the weight of the evidence "decisively" supported the view that two-parent families are better than single-parent families.

Decisively to him, perhaps, but not to others. Judith Stacey, another professor of sociology, responded in a letter to the *Times* that the value of a two-parent family was merely "a widely shared prejudice" not confirmed by empirical studies; Popenoe, she said, was trying to convert "misguided nostalgia for 'Ozzie-and-Harriet'-land into social-scientific truth." Arlene and Jerome Skolnick, two more professors, acknowledged that although Popenoe might be correct, saying so publicly would "needlessly stigmatize children raised in families that don't meet the 'Ozzie-and-Harriet' model."

...

Barbara Dafoe Whitehead recently surveyed the most prominent textbooks on marriage and the family. Here is my paraphrase of her summary of what she found:

> The life course is full of exciting options. These include living in a commune, having a group marriage, being a single parent, or living together. Marriage is one life-style choice, but before choosing it people weigh its costs and benefits against other options. Divorce is a part of the normal family cycle and is neither deviant nor tragic. Rather, it can serve as a foundation for individual renewal and new beginnings. Marriage itself should not be regarded as a special, privileged institution; on the contrary, it must catch up with the diverse, pluralistic society in which we live. For example, same-sex marriages often involve more sharing and equality than do heterosexual relationships. But even in the conventional family, the relationships between husband and wife need to be defined after carefully negotiating agreements that protect each person's separate interests and rights.

Many politicians and reporters echo these sentiments and carry the argument one step further. Not only do poor Ozzie and Harriet (surely the most maligned figures in the history of television) stand for nostalgic prejudice and stigmatizing error, they represent a kind of family that in fact scarcely exists. [Former] Congresswoman Pat Schroeder has been quoted as saying that only about 7 percent of all American families fit the Ozzie-and-Harriet model. Our daily newspapers frequently assert that most children will not grow up in a two-parent family. The message is clear: Not only is the two-parent family not especially good for children, but fortunately it is also fast disappearing.

...

The proponents of the relic theory fail to use statistics accurately. The way they arrive at the discovery that only 7 percent of all families fit the Ozzie-and-Harriet model is by calculating what proportion of all families consists exactly of a father, mother, and two (not three or four) children and in which the mother never works, not even for two weeks during the year helping out with the Christmas rush at the post office.

The language in which the debate over two-parent families is carried on suggests that something more than scholarly uncertainty is at stake. If all we cared about were the effects of one- versus two-parent families on the lives of children, there would still be a debate, but it would not be conducted on op-ed pages in tones of barely controlled anger. Nor would it be couched in slogans about television characters or supported by misleading statistics.

What is at stake, of course, is the role of women. To defend the two-parent family is to defend, the critics worry, an institution in which the woman is subordinated to her husband, confined to domestic chores with no opportunity to pursue a career, and taught to indoctrinate her children with a belief in the rightness of this arrangement. To some critics, the woman here is not simply constrained, she is abused. The traditional family, in this view, is an arena in which men are free to hit, rape, and exploit women. To defend the traditional family is to defend sexism. And since single-parent families are disproportionately headed by black women, criticizing such families is not only sexist but racist.

Perhaps the most influential book on this subject to appear during the 1970s was *The Future of Marriage* by Jessie Bernard, a distinguished scholar. Widely reviewed, its central message was that the first order of business for marriage must be "mitigating its hazards for women."

Unlike more radical writers, Bernard thought that the future of marriage was assured, but this would be the case only because marriage would now take many forms. Traditional marriages would persist but other forms would gain (indeed, had already gained) favor—communes, group marriages, the *ménage à trois*, marital "swinging," unmarried cohabitation, and limited-commitment marriages. (She did not discuss mother-only families as one of these "options." Nor did she discuss race.) In principle, no one form was better than another because "there is nothing in human nature that favors one kind of marriage over another." In practice, the forms that were best were those that were best for the woman. What might be best for children was not discussed. Children, it would seem, were incidental to marriage, except insofar as their care imposed strains on their parents, especially their mothers.

The main theme of much of the writing about marriage and families during the 1970s and 1980s was that of individual rights. Just as polities were only legitimate when they respected individual rights, so also marriages were worthy of respect only when they were based on a recognition of rights.

...

Family—and kinship generally—are the fundamental organizing facts of all human societies, primitive or advanced, and have been such for tens of thousands of years. The family is the product of evolutionary processes that have selected against people who are inclined to abandon their offspring and for people who are prepared to care for them, and to provide this caring within kinship systems defined primarily along genetic lines. If kinship were a cultural artifact, we could as easily define it on the basis of height, athletic skill, or political status, and children would be raised in all manner of collectives, ranging from state-run orphanages to market-supplied foster homes. Orphanages and foster homes do of course exist, but only as matters of last resort designed (with great public anxiety) to provide care when the biological family does not exist or cannot function.

If the family were merely a convenience and if it responded entirely to economic circumstances, the current debate over family policy would be far less rancorous than it is. Liberals would urge that we professionalize child rearing through day care; conservatives would urge that we subsidize it through earned-income tax credits. Liberals would define the welfare problem as entirely a matter of poverty and recommend more generous benefits as the solution; conservatives would define it as entirely a matter of dependency and recommend slashing benefits as the solution. Liberals would assume that the problem is that families have too little money, conservatives that families get such money as they have from the state. There would still be a battle, but in the end it would come down to some negotiated compromise involving trade-offs among benefit levels, eligibility rules, and the public-private mix of child-care providers.

But once one conceives of the family problem as involving to a significant degree the conflict between a universal feature of human society and a profound cultural challenge to the power of that institution, the issue takes on a different character. To the extent that one believes in the cultural challenge—that is, in individual emancipation and individual choice—one tends to question the legitimacy and influence of the family. To the extent that one believes in the family, one is led to question some or all parts of the cultural challenge.

That is why the debate over "family values" has been so strident. On both sides people feel that it is the central battle in the culture war that now grips Americans (or at least American elites). They are absolutely right. To many liberals, family values means a reassertion of male authority, a reduction in the hard-earned rights of women, and a license for abusive or neglectful parents to mistreat their children free of prompt and decisive social intervention. For some liberals, family values means something even more troubling: that human nature is less malleable than is implied by the doctrine of environmental determinism and cultural relativism—that it is to some significant degree fixed, immutable. To many conservatives, family values is the main line of resistance against homosexual marriages, bureaucratized child care, and compulsory sex education in the schools. For some conservatives, the family means a defense against the very idea of a planned society.

...

On one issue most parents will squarely identify with the conservative side, and it is, in my view, the central issue. They will want our leaders, the media, television programs, and motion pictures to take their side in the war over what the family is. It is not one of several alternative lifestyles; it is not an arena in which rights are negotiated; it is not an old-fashioned and reactionary barrier to a promiscuous sex life; it is not a set of cost-benefit calculations. It is a commitment.

It is a commitment required for child rearing and thus for any realistic prospect of human happiness. It is a commitment that may be entered into after romantic experimentation and with some misgivings about lost freedoms, but once entered into it is a commitment that persists for richer or for poorer, in sickness and in health, for better or for worse. It is a commitment for which there is no feasible substitute, and hence no child ought lightly to be brought into a world where that commitment—from both parents—is absent. It is a commitment that often is joyfully enlivened by mutual love and deepening friendship, but it is a commitment even when these things are absent.

There is no way to prepare for the commitment other than to make it. The idea that a man and a woman can live together without a commitment in order to see if they would like each other after they make the commitment is preposterous. Living together may inform you as to whether your partner snores or is an alcoholic or sleeps late; it may be fun and exciting; it may even be the best you can manage in an imperfect world. But it is not a way of finding out how married life will be, because married life is shaped by the fact that the couple has made a solemn vow before their family and friends that this is for keeps and that any children will be their joint and permanent responsibility. It changes everything.

Despite high divorce rates and a good deal of sleeping around, most people understand this. Certainly women understand it, since one of their most common complaints about the men they know is that they will not make a commitment. You bet they won't, not if they can get sex, cooking, and companionship on a trial basis, all the while keeping their eyes peeled for a better opportunity elsewhere. Marriage is in large measure a device for reining in the predatory sexuality of males. It works quite imperfectly, as is evident from the fact that men are more likely than women to have extramarital affairs and to abandon their spouses because a younger or more exciting possibility has presented herself. But it works better than anything else mankind has been able to invent.

Because most people understand this, the pressures, economic and cultural, on the modern family have not destroyed it. And this is remarkable, considering the spread of no-fault divorce laws. The legal system has, in effect, said, "Marriage is not a commitment; it is a convenience. If you feel yours is inconvenient, we will make it easy for you to get out of it."

...

These cultural and legal changes, all aimed at individualizing and empowering family members, have had an effect. In 1951, 51 percent of all Americans agreed with the statement that "parents who don't get along should not stay together because there are children in the family." By 1985, 86 percent agreed. Still, these changes have not devastated modern families. The shopping malls, baseball stadiums, and movie theaters are filled with them doing what families have always done. That fact is a measure of the innate power of the family bond.

...

When the people who deliver mocking attacks on "traditional family values" are the same ones who endorse condom distribution among elementary-school children, the average parent is led to wonder whether he or she is being a sucker for trying to stay together and raise the kids. Most Americans, I would guess, understand very clearly the difference between a traditional family and an oppressive one; they want the former but not the latter. Most women, I would guess, can distinguish very easily between the rights they have won and the obligations they retain; they cherish both and see no fundamental conflict between them, except the inescapable problem that there is not enough time for everything and so everyone must make choices.

It is extraordinary how well most husbands and wives have held up in the face of constant taunts comparing them to Ozzie and Harriet. The family life that most Americans want is regarded by the eminences of the media and the academy as a cartoon life, fit only for ridicule and rejection. When the history of our times is written, this raging cultural war will deserve careful attention, for it is far more consequential than any of the other cleavages that divide us.

The American Family and the Nostalgia Trap

Stephanie
Coontz

... At the risk of being branded some kind of moral monster who favors parental irresponsibility, beats up on the beleaguered two-parent family, and spits in the face of common sense, I want to argue that the revival of the family values crusade poses serious dangers for people who sincerely want to improve the lives of American children. Of course values are important, and of course there are some truly awful parental behaviors and family dynamics out there. But polarizing the issue as their bad values versus our good ones or their bad parenting versus our commitment to kids ignores the fact that all of us have bad values as well as good ones. It vastly underestimates the role of external environments and institutions in reinforcing some values while extinguishing others and in letting some people get away with periodic lapses of personal responsibility while others pay dearly and permanently for even the smallest mistake. It also leads to unnecessary pessimism about the prospects for some families and unwarranted complacency about the prospects for others.

Beneath the seemingly sensible claim that the "breakdown of the family" causes all our social ills lies a simplistic analysis of how traditional family forms and gender roles used to operate, of where contemporary family problems originate, and of what parents can and should do to raise healthy children in the 1990s. And where oversimplified analysis occurs, bad policy and punitive moralism are sure to follow. For if family breakdown is the central problem of our age, what is the solution?

...

From *Phi Delta Kappan* 76, no. 7 (March 1995). Copyright © 1995. Reprinted with the permission of Phi Delta Kappa International and the author.

Whatever its virtues, marriage is hardly a social program or an adequate substitute for structural economic and political reform. How could we implement a "policy" of solving poverty through marriage? Family values crusaders have discussed making divorce harder for couples with children, but no one has figured out how to do that without trapping people in truly poisonous families or exacerbating the parental conflicts that are associated with the worst outcomes for children. So a "values revolution" is proposed instead.

...

Only in the 1950s did large numbers of Americans begin to identify the nuclear family as the "fount of virtue, spring of wealth," main source of childhood socialization, and center of all personal happiness. During the Great Depression and World War II, millions of Americans doubled up in housing or moved in with parents, and millions more were parted from spouse and children. Murder rates in the 1930s were higher than in the 1980s. Marriage rates reached an all-time high in 1946, but by 1948, one in every three new marriages was ending in divorce. Relief at the end of World War II gave way to deep anxieties about the Bomb, while the Canwell Committee and Senator Joseph McCarthy led a massive witch hunt into people's political associations. Having had the wrong friend at the wrong time could lose a job or destroy a reputation.

In these circumstances, community institutions, extended families, and same-sex peer groups began to lose their luster. In contrast, the nuclear family began to seem a welcome refuge, a potential oasis of security, if marriage could only be made more stable. Amid the extraordinary consumerism unleashed by the postwar economic boom, the prospects seemed bright for finding new comforts, both material and emotional, in the home.

An unprecedented emotional and spatial rearrangement of family life occurred in the 1950s, as everyone from family therapists to real estate agents and from automobile advertisers to movie script writers urged young couples to move away from parents and kin and cut ties with old networks of friends and neighbors who might compete for emotional attention. The new ideal was to wean couples away from traditional extra-familial networks, encouraging them to focus all their energies and find all their gratifications within the home.

At the time, everyone knew that the families we now watch nostalgically on "Nick at Night" did not represent the way it really was, but rather the way many hoped it might be. The sitcoms were testimonials and how-to lessons for a new way of organizing gender and age roles. Indeed, they might be seen as the 1950s equivalent of today's beer ads. Just as most beer ads are consciously aimed at men who aren't as strong and sexy as those in the commercials, the happy-family sitcoms were aimed at young couples who had married in haste, women who had tasted new freedoms during World War II and given up their jobs with regret, and returning veterans whose children often resented their attempts to assert paternal authority. The message was clear: Buy these ranch houses, appliances, and new child-rearing ideals; relate to your spouse like this; organize your dinner like that—and you too can have harmonious families in which father knows best, mother is never bored, and the teenagers are always eager to hear words of parental wisdom.

If the decade of the 1950s was the "heyday" of the nuclear family, it was also a historical aberration. At the tail end of the 1940s, for the first time in 100 years, the average age of marriage and parenthood fell, the proportion of marriages ending in divorce dropped, and the birth rate "approached that of India." The percentage of women remaining childless reached an all-time low, while the timing and spacing of childbearing became far more compressed, so that young women were likely to have two or more children in diapers at the same time, without an older sibling to help in their care.

At the same time, and again for the first time in 100 years, the educational gap between middle-class women and men increased, while the employment gap between non-college-bound male and female teens peaked. These demographic changes (in contrast to gradual trends in the opposite direction since the early twentieth century) increased the dependence of young women on marriage. All these innovations lasted approximately 10 years. By 1958 the older and long-term trends began to reassert themselves.

Fluke or not, say the "new traditionalists," the 1950s stand as a model for what family values can accomplish. In the 1950s stable marriages and devoted parenting fostered personal and social security, national prosperity, and a strong work ethic. We can regain those traits if we revive the 1950s family and its moral precepts—perhaps throwing in just a little more independence for women along the way.

But history does not support such a hopeful scenario. Low rates of divorce and unwed motherhood in the 1950s did not prevent 30 percent of American children from living in poverty, a higher figure than today's. Married African-American couples had a poverty rate of nearly 50 percent. Many "traditional" families of the 1950s were hardly idyllic, as thousands of survivors of alcoholic dysfunction, abuse, battering, or incest can testify. Women and blacks were denied the most fundamental economic, educational, and legal rights. One reason people worried less in the 1950s was that few of these problems made the nightly news. They were either taken for granted or systematically covered up.

It is true that many families had more hopeful economic prospects than they do today. Poverty declined steadily from 1939 through the mid-1960s, while rates of home ownership rose and rates of unemployment fell. And many middle-aged Americans remember growing up in harmonious 1950s families where they were sheltered from the ravages of poverty and the fear of violence.

...

But the social stability of the 1950s was less a result of that decade's family forms or values than of its unique socioeconomic and political climate. High rates of unionization, heavy corporate investment in manufacturing plants and equipment, and generous government assistance in the form of public works projects, veterans' benefits, student loans, and housing subsidies gave young families a tremendous economic jump start, created predictable paths out of poverty, and led to unprecedented increases in real wages. In both the 1950s and 1960s, by the time the average man reached the age of 30, he could pay the principal and the interest on a median-priced home with only 15 percent to 18 percent of his income. (In 1983, the same feat took 40 percent.)

...

Both conservatives and liberals tend to forget how much family values and effective child rearing depend on a supportive economic and social environment. You can't suck self-esteem out of your thumb, nor can you beat it into people's heads, no matter how many inspirational seminars or parenting classes you take.

In the socioeconomic environment of the 1950s, even children who had grown up in dysfunctional families could succeed. When the children of 1950s families reached adulthood in the 1970s, however, they faced quite a different economic and political climate. It was the children of the stable families formed in the 1950s, the recipients of so much parental time and attention, who pioneered the sharp breaks with traditional family arrangements in the 1970s.

Was this because of a values revolution? Partly. Some of that revolution was long overdue—for example, the notion that women should have options in the public world. Some of it was a logical extension of the materialistic individualism encouraged by the privatized, depoliticized values glorified in the 1950s. Some was a rebellion against what young people saw as the hypocrisy of their parents, who preached personal morality but ignored such social evils as racism and war. And many cultural changes came from Madison Avenue's efforts to co-opt the youth rebellion.

But the structural constraints under which people developed and prioritized these new values were laid down by new socioeconomic trends that clashed with all the expectations that 1950s families had instilled in their children. That clash, not the willful abandonment of responsibility and commitment, has been the primary cause both of family rearrangements and of the growing social problems that are usually attributed to such family changes (but which in fact have separate origins).

To evaluate the gains, losses, trade-offs, and alternative outcomes of family change over the past three decades and to help families make the best choices they can in their new situations, we must understand that, contrary to myth, people's "lifestyle choices" and family transitions are not the foremost causes of such problems as poverty, crime, educational failure, and personal dysfunction.

...

A society that hopes to foster personal responsibility to others must convince its members that they share some connectedness, that their fortunes are somehow bound together. But it's hard to make people believe that today. Real wages have been falling for most Americans since 1973 (and for young workers since 1967). For a while, in the late 1960s and early 1970s, poverty continued to decline, thanks largely to the Great Society programs that it has become so fashionable to trash. But since the mid-1970s, both absolute and relative poverty have grown steadily, with inequality reaching ever new heights. Even after taxes, the top 20 percent of American families now rake in 44 percent of total income (not counting capital gains from the sale of homes, cars, stocks, and bonds); the bottom 20 percent must get by on 3.9 percent. And this astonishingly small share includes the cash value of food stamps and other benefits for the poor! In fact, the top 1 percent of the population has as much income as the entire bottom 40 percent.

...

Lamentations about the "collapse of the family" and prescriptions for revitalizing society through people's personal commitments to family life divert our attention from this larger deterioration in the social ecology. Even if we ignore the repressive elements of the new family crusade and endorse its absolutely correct call for greater commitment to children, America needs more than a family system based on reciprocity and obligation. As business writer Bob Kuttner has commented, it also "needs an economy based upon notions of mutual obligation and reciprocity."

...

The problem is that such seemingly innocuous generalizations encourage preconceived notions that a particular "intact" family does have a responsible, involved mother and father and that a particular single-parent or reconstituted family does not have its own strengths. People end up in single-parent homes for a variety of reasons, some of which even the most radical right-wingers would acknowledge as valid. And there is much wider variation among children from single-parent families, including never-married ones, than there is between the averages for each category.

...

Certainly, one-parent families face serious challenges. After all, it's hard enough for two parents to raise children in a society in which rampant consumerism is constantly rubbing against rampant inequality. But most families can meet the challenges, so long as these are not multiplied by intense economic stress, deteriorating social support systems, and the very same social stigma that the family values crusaders believe to be part of the cure for our family problems. Indeed, one review of the literature on single-parent families found that the only situations in which children of one-parent families suffered losses of self-esteem were those in which single-parent families were stigmatized.

...

Children stuck in high-conflict marriages or ones in which a father is angry and withdrawn often have worse long-term problems than children in single-parent families. One recent study of adolescent self-esteem found no differences by family structure. However, the lowest self-esteem of all groups was found in teens of two-parent families whose fathers had low levels of interest in them. Such youngsters, lacking even the excuse of the father's absence to explain his disengagement, were more likely to blame themselves for their father's lack of interest. It is also more possible for two-parent families to hide problems of abuse, incest, and alcoholism from the outside world than it is for one-parent families.

Even harmonious couples need to beware of certain pitfalls. Thinking themselves complete and self-sufficient, they may not give their children enough exposure to experiences and values that differ from their own. Such families occasionally foster an inward orientation that hinders a child from striking out in new directions or learning to appreciate difference in others.

Key Websites

DIVORCE AND THE FAMILY IN AMERICA

Christopher Lasch, "Divorce and the Family in America": In this historically interesting article from the November 1966 issue of the *Atlantic Monthly*, Christopher Lasch speculates that it is quite possible that easier divorce, far from threatening the family, will actually help to preserve it as a dominant institution of modern society. He notes that only alarmists would argue that the family is literally becoming extinct. He believes divorce reform will be accompanied by dire predictions of the disintegration of domestic values, but points out that the family has outlived such predictions before. The idea that the family is a sacred cornerstone of society is a characteristically modern idea. He believes that the family will not be threatened by the increase in divorces.

http://www.theatlantic.com/politics/family/divorce.htm

THE BREAKDOWN OF THE FAMILY—THE CONSEQUENCES FOR CHILDREN AND AMERICAN SOCIETY

Patrick F. Fagan (Heritage Foundation), "The Breakdown of the Family—The Consequences for Children and American Society": This report includes information supporting the view that divorce and father-absence are major problems that must be reversed.

http://www.acfc.org/study/fagan.pdf

DIVORCE REFORM: AN IDEA WHOSE TIME IS COMING

David M. Wagner, "Divorce Reform: An Idea Whose Time Is Coming": Wagner claims that the no-fault revolution that swept through the states from the late 1960s through the early 1980s with virtually no public airing of the issues seemed to have silenced any and all opposition. Today, the momentum is toward reducing our high divorce rate, providing more security to spouses and children, and restoring to marrying couples the one freedom that the no-fault revolution took away—the freedom to make a binding commitment. Marriages, like business partnerships, don't work out automatically. They require heavy investments, by both parties, of time, effort, and otherwise-permissible enjoyments foregone.

http://www.frc.org/fampol/fp97ims.html

CHILDSTATS

This site gives easy access to federal and state statistics and reports on children and their families, including population and family characteristics and economic security.

http://www.childstats.gov

THE MADNESS OF THE AMERICAN FAMILY

Midge Decter, "The Madness of the American Family," *Policy Review* (September–October 1998): Author and social critic Midge Decter asks why the wealthiest and healthiest country on earth has developed what she feels are extremely destructive ideas about the family.
http://www.policyreview.com/sept98/family.html

CHILDREN'S DEFENSE FUND

The Children's Defense Fund exists to provide a strong and effective voice for all the children of America. The organization pays particular attention to the needs of poor and minority children and to children with disabilities. Its goal is to educate the nation about the needs of children.
http://www.childrensdefense.org

WOMEN'S EMPLOYMENT AND CARE OF CHILDREN IN THE UNITED STATES

Sandra L. Hofferth, Institute for Social Research, University of Michigan, "Women's Employment and Care of Children in the United States": This paper addresses the question of the relationship between the employment of women and the access of children to parental care and attention. Data were drawn from a national survey of U.S. children under age 13 conducted in 1997. The study found that children whose mother was employed had less access to her time than children in families where the mother was not employed outside the home. However, this did not significantly reduce the amount of time the mother spent with the child. Children also spend more time with their fathers when mothers work.
http://www.ethno.isr.umich.edu/papers/ceel003-99.pdf

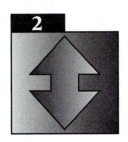

Has Fatherhood Been Devalued?

The fall 1992 season premiere of the CBS program *Murphy Brown* assumed the proportions of what the *New York Times* called a national event. Earlier in the year, the show's main character, Murphy Brown, had decided to bear a child outside of marriage, thus becoming a single mother by choice. When then-vice president Dan Quayle criticized the show for mocking the importance of fathers, a protracted national controversy erupted, in which Quayle was roundly and repeatedly denounced. In the season-opening episode, watched by a remarkable 41 percent of that night's television audience, Murphy took her revenge, rebuking Quayle on the air for his painfully unfair remark about the necessity of fathers and reminding viewers that families come in all shapes and sizes.

In a reversal from previous decades, many Americans now believe it is acceptable for a woman to choose to have and raise a child on her own, without the involvement of a father. A survey by Voter/Consumer Research (1993) found that 70 percent of people aged 18 to 34 endorsed the proposition that it is morally acceptable to have children outside of marriage.

Increases in divorce and out-of-wedlock childbearing have dramatically altered the family life of American children. Whereas in the early 1960s nearly 90 percent of all children lived with both biological parents until they reached adulthood, today fewer than half of children grow up with both natural parents. Nearly a third are born to unmarried mothers, the majority of whom never live with the father. Another third are born to married parents who eventually divorce. Making matters worse, many children are exposed to multiple marital disruptions and multiple father figures.

These changes have created tremendous uncertainty in children's lives and have led to considerable speculation about the consequences of father absence. Some people claim that growing up in a fatherless home is the main cause of child poverty, delinquency, and school failure. Others have denied that single motherhood has any harmful effects and argue that poverty and economic insecurity are the real culprits, causing both father absence and teenage behavior problems.

Some observers maintain that the United States is being divided into two groups, separate and unequal. One group receives basic benefits—psychological, social, economic, educational, and moral—that are denied to the other group. The line dividing the two groups, say these observers, is the daily presence of a father.

David Popenoe, in "A World without Fathers," contends that "the decline of fatherhood is one of the most basic, unexpected, and extraordinary social trends of our time." He thinks that the current generation of children may be the first in our nation's history to be less well off psychologically, socially, and economically than their parents were. As this situation unfolds he is surprised to see our cultural view of fatherhood also change. Few people doubt the fundamental importance of mothers, but many question whether fathers are really necessary.

Louise B. Silverstein and Carl F. Auerbach, in their essay "Deconstructing the Essential Father," note that neither the father nor the mother is essential in a family. Their research with divorced, never-married, and remarried fathers has led them to conclude that a wide variety of family structures can support positive child outcomes. They think that a child needs at least one responsible, caretaking adult who has a positive, stable emotional connection with him or her. This person—who may or may not be the father or mother—can be found in a variety of settings—it might be in a single-parent household, with a gay or lesbian couple, or in a larger grouping. Predictability and a consistent relationship are the important factors, not gender or biological relationship.

Yes

A World without Fathers

David
Popenoe

The decline of fatherhood is one of the most basic, unexpected, and extraordinary social trends of our time. Its dimensions can be captured in a single statistic: In just three decades, between 1960 and 1990, the percentage of children living apart from their biological fathers more than doubled, from 17 percent to 36 percent. By the turn of the century, nearly 50 percent of American children may be going to sleep each evening without being able to say good night to their dads.

No one predicted this trend, few researchers or government agencies have monitored it, and it is not widely discussed, even today. But the decline of fatherhood is a major force behind many of the most disturbing problems that plague American society: crime and delinquency; premature sexuality and out-of-wedlock births to teenagers; deteriorating educational achievement; depression, substance abuse, and alienation among adolescents; and the growing number of women and children in poverty.

The current generation of children and youth may be the first in our nation's history to be less well off—psychologically, socially, economically, and morally—than their parents were at the same age....

Even as this calamity unfolds, our cultural view of fatherhood itself is changing. Few people doubt the fundamental importance of mothers. But fathers? More and more, the question of whether fathers are really necessary is being raised. Many would answer no, or maybe not. And to the degree that fathers are still thought necessary, fatherhood is said by many to be merely a social role that others can play: mothers, partners, stepfathers, uncles and aunts, grandparents. Perhaps the script can even be rewritten and the role changed—or dropped.

There was a time in the past when fatherlessness was far more common than it is today, but death was to blame, not divorce, desertion, and out-of-wedlock births. In early-seventeenth-century Virginia, only an estimated 31 percent of white children reached age 18 with both parents still alive. That percentage climbed to 50 percent by the early eighteenth century, to 72 percent by the turn of the present century, and close to its current level by 1940. Today, well over 90 percent of America's youngsters reach 18 with two living parents. Almost all of today's fatherless children have fathers who are alive, well, and perfectly capable of shouldering the responsibilities of fatherhood. Who would ever have thought that so many men would choose to relinquish them?

Not so long ago, the change in the cause of fatherlessness was dismissed as irrelevant in many quarters, including among social scientists. Children, it was said, are merely losing their parents in a different way than they used to. You don't hear that very much anymore. A surprising finding of recent social science research is that it is decidedly worse for a child to lose a father in the modern, voluntary way than through death. The children of divorced and never-married mothers are less successful in life by almost every measure than the children of widowed mothers. The replacement of death by divorce as the prime cause of fatherlessness, then, is a monumental setback in the history of childhood.

Until the 1960s, the falling death rate and the rising divorce rate neutralized each other. In 1900, the percentage of all American children living in single-parent families was 8.5 percent. By 1960, it had increased to just 9.1 percent. Virtually no one during those years was writing or thinking about family breakdown, disintegration, or decline.

Indeed, what is most significant about the changing family demography of the first six decades of the twentieth century is this: Because the death rate was dropping faster than the divorce rate was rising, by 1960 more children were living with both of their natural parents than at any other time in world history. The figure was close to 80 percent for the generation born in the late 1940s and early 1950s.

But then the decline in the death rate slowed, and the divorce rate skyrocketed. "The scale of marital breakdowns in the West since 1960 has no historical precedent that I know of, and seems unique," says Lawrence Stone, the noted Princeton University family historian. "There has been nothing like it for the last 2,000 years, and probably longer."

Consider what has happened to children. Most estimates are that only about 50 percent of the children born during the 1970–84 "baby bust" period will still live with their natural parents by age 17—a staggering drop from nearly 80 percent.

...

The picture grows worse. Just as divorce has overtaken death as the leading cause of fatherlessness, out-of-wedlock births are expected to surpass divorce later in the 1990s. They accounted for 30 percent of all births by 1991; by the turn of the century they may account for 40 percent of the total (and 80 percent of minority births). And there is substantial evidence that having an unmarried father is even worse for a child than having a divorced father.

Across time and cultures, fathers have always been considered essential—and not just for their sperm. Indeed, until today, no known society ever thought of fathers as potentially unnecessary. Marriage and the nuclear family—mother, father, and children—are the most universal social institutions in existence. In no society has the birth of children out of wedlock been the cultural norm. To the contrary, a concern for the legitimacy of children is nearly universal.

At the same time, being a father is universally problematic for men. While mothers the world over bear and nurture their young with an intrinsic acknowledgment and, most commonly, acceptance of their role, the process of taking on the role of father is often filled with conflict and doubt. The source of this sex-role difference can be plainly stated. Men are not biologically as attuned to being committed fathers as women are to being committed mothers. The evolutionary logic is clear. Women, who can bear only a limited number of children, have a great incentive to invest their energy in rearing children, while men, who can father many offspring, do not. Left culturally unregulated, men's sexual behavior can be promiscuous, their paternity casual, their commitment to families weak. This is not to say that the role of father is foreign to male nature. Far from it. Evolutionary scientists tell us that the development of the fathering capacity and high paternal investments in offspring—features not common among our primate relatives—have been sources of enormous evolutionary advantage for human beings.

In recognition of the fatherhood problem, human cultures have used sanctions to bind men to their children, and of course the institution of marriage has been culture's chief vehicle. Marriage is society's way of signaling that the community approves and encourages sexual intercourse and the birth of children, and that the long-term relationship of the parents is socially important. Margaret Mead once said, with the fatherhood problem very much in mind, that there is no society in the world where men will stay married for very long unless culturally required to do so. Our experience in late-twentieth-century America shows how right she was. The results for children have been devastating.

In my many years as a sociologist, I have found few other bodies of evidence that lean so much in one direction as this one: On the whole, two parents—a father and a mother—are better for a child than one parent. There are, to be sure, many factors that complicate this simple proposition.

We all know of a two-parent family that is truly dysfunctional—the prover-bial family from hell. A child can certainly be raised to a fulfilling adulthood by one loving parent who is wholly devoted to the child's well-being. But such exceptions do not invalidate the rule any more than the fact that some three-pack-a-day smokers live to a ripe old age casts doubt on the dangers of cigarettes.

...

The most tangible and immediate consequence of fatherlessness for children is the loss of economic resources. By the best recent estimates, the income of the household in which a child remains after a divorce instantly declines by about 21 percent per capita on average, while expenses tend to go up. Over time, the economic situation for the child often deteriorates fur-ther. The mother usually earns considerably less than the father, and chil-dren cannot rely on their fathers to pay much in the way of child support. About half of previously married mothers receive no child support, and for those who do receive it, both the reliability and the amount of the payment drop over time.

...

What do fathers do? Much of what they contribute to the growth of their children, of course, is simply the result of being a second adult in the home. Bringing up children is demanding, stressful, and often exhausting. Two adults can not only support and spell each other; they can offset each other's deficiencies and build on each other's strengths.

Beyond being merely a second adult or third party, fathers/men bring an array of unique and irreplaceable qualities that women do not ordinari-ly bring. Some of these are familiar, if sometimes overlooked or taken for granted. The father as protector, for example, has by no means outlived his usefulness. His importance as a role model has become a familiar idea. Teenage boys without fathers are notoriously prone to trouble. The pathway to adulthood for daughters is somewhat easier, but they still must learn from their fathers, as they cannot from their mothers, how to relate to men. They learn from their fathers about heterosexual trust, intimacy, and differ-ence. They learn to appreciate their own femininity from the one male who is most special in their lives (assuming that they love and respect their fathers). Most important, through loving and being loved by their fathers, they learn that they are love-worthy.

...

At play and in other realms, fathers tend to stress competition, chal-lenge, initiative, risk taking, and independence. Mothers, as caretakers, stress emotional security and personal safety. On the playground, fathers will try to get the child to swing ever higher, higher than the person on the next swing, while mothers will be cautious, worrying about an accident. It's sometimes said that fathers express more concern for the child's longer-term develop-ment, while mothers focus on the child's immediate well-being (which, of course, in its own way has everything to do with a child's long-term well-being). What is clear is that children have dual needs that must be met. Becoming a mature and competent adult involves the integration of two often-contradictory human desires: for communion, or the feeling of being included, connected, and related, and for agency, which entails independence, individuality, and self-fulfillment. One without the other is a denuded and impaired humanity, an incomplete realization of human potential.

...

We know, however, that fathers—and fatherlessness—have surprising impacts on children. Fathers' involvement seems to be linked to improved quantitative and verbal skills, improved problem-solving ability, and higher academic achievement. Several studies have found that the presence of the father is one of the determinants of girls' proficiency in mathematics. And one pioneering study found that the amount of time fathers spent reading was a strong predictor of their daughters' verbal ability.

...

Men also have a vital role to play in promoting cooperation and other "soft" virtues. We don't often think of fathers in connection with the teaching of empathy, but involved fathers, it turns out, may be of special importance for the development of this important character trait, essential to an ordered society of law-abiding, cooperative, and compassionate adults. Examining the results of a 26-year longitudinal study, a trio of researchers reached a "quite astonishing" conclusion: The most important childhood factor of all in developing empathy is paternal involvement in child care. Fathers who spent time alone with their children more than twice a week, giving meals, baths, and other basic care, reared the most compassionate adults.

Again, it is not yet clear why fathers are so important in instilling this quality. Perhaps merely by being with their children they provide a model for compassion. Perhaps it has to do with their style of play or mode of reasoning. Perhaps it is somehow related to the fact that fathers typically are the family's main arbiter with the outside world. Or perhaps it is because mothers who receive help from their mates have more time and energy to cultivate the soft virtues. Whatever the reason, it is hard to think of a more important contribution that fathers can make to their children.

...

Marriage by itself, even without the presence of children, is also a major civilizing force for men. No other institution save religion (and perhaps the military) places such moral demands on men. To be sure, there is a selection factor in marriage. Those men whom women would care to marry already have some of the civilized virtues. And those men who are morally beyond the pale have difficulty finding mates. Yet epidemiological studies and social surveys have shown that marriage has a civilizing effect independent of the selection factor. Marriage actually promotes health, competence, virtue, and personal well-being. With the continued growth of fatherlessness, we can expect to see a nation of men who are at worst morally out of control and at best unhappy, unhealthy, and unfulfilled.

Just as cultural forms can be discarded, dismantled, and declared obsolete, so can they be reinvented. In order to restore marriage and reinstate fathers in the lives of their children, we are somehow going to have to undo the cultural shift of the last few decades toward radical individualism. We are going to have to reembrace some cultural propositions or understandings that throughout history have been universally accepted but which today are unpopular, if not rejected outright.

Marriage must be reestablished as a strong social institution. The father's role must also be redefined in a way that neglects neither historical models nor the unique attributes of modern societies, the new roles for women, and the special qualities that men bring to child rearing.

…

Today in America the social order is fraying badly. We seem, despite notable accomplishments in some areas, to be on a path of decline. The past three decades have seen steeply rising rates of crime, declining political and interpersonal trust, growing personal and corporate greed, deteriorating communities, and increasing confusion over moral issues. For most Americans, life has become more anxious, unsettled, and insecure.

…

At the heart of our discontent lies an erosion of personal relationships. People no longer trust others as they once did; they no longer feel the same sense of commitment and obligation to others. In part, this may be an unavoidable product of the modern condition. But it has gone much deeper than that. Some children across America now go to bed each night worrying about whether their father will be there the next morning. Some wonder whatever happened to their father. And some wonder who he is. What are these children learning at this most basic of all levels about honesty, self-sacrifice, personal responsibility, and trust?

What the decline of fatherhood and marriage in America really means, then, is that slowly, insidiously, and relentlessly our society has been moving in an ominous direction. If we are to make progress toward a more just and humane society, we must reverse the tide that is pulling fathers apart from their families. Nothing is more important for our children or for our future as a nation.

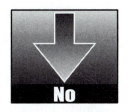

Deconstructing
the Essential Father

Louise B.
Silverstein
and Carl F.
Auerbach

In the past two decades, there has been an explosion of research on fathers (see Booth and Crouter, 1998; Lamb, 1997; Phares, 1996, for recent reviews). There is now a broad consensus that fathers are important contributors to both normal and abnormal child outcomes. Infants and toddlers can be as attached to fathers as they are to mothers. In addition, even when fathers are not physically present, they may play an important role in their children's psychological lives.

...

Overall, this explosion of research on fathering has increased the complexity of scholarly thinking about parenting and child development. However, one group of social scientists (e.g., Biller and Kimpton, 1997; Blankenhorn, 1995; Popenoe, 1996) has emerged that is offering a more simplistic view of the role of fathers in families. These neoconservative social scientists have replaced the earlier "essentializing" of mothers (Bowlby, 1951) with a claim about the essential importance of fathers. These authors have proposed that the roots of a wide range of social problems (i.e., child poverty, urban decay, societal violence, teenage pregnancy, and poor school performance) can be traced to the absence of fathers in the lives of their children.

...

We characterize this perspective as essentialist because it assumes that the biologically different reproductive functions of men and women automatically construct essential differences in parenting behaviors. The essentialist perspective defines mothering and fathering as distinct social roles that are not interchangeable. Marriage is seen as the social institution within which responsible fathering and positive child adjustment are most likely to occur. Fathers are understood as having a unique and essential role to play in child development, especially for boys who need a male role model to establish a masculine gender identity (see Table 1 for a definition of the essentialist perspective).

Our research experience has led us to conceptualize fathering in a way that is very different from the neoconservative perspective.

···

In contrast to the neoconservative perspective, our data on gay fathering couples have convinced us that neither a mother nor a father is essential. Similarly, our research with divorced, never-married, and remarried fathers has taught us that a wide variety of family structures can support positive child outcomes. We have concluded that children need at least one

Table 1   The Essentialist Paradigm

Essentialist Belief	Explanation
Biological sex differences construct gender differences in parenting	The biological experiences of pregnancy and lactation generate a strong, instinctual drive in women to nurture. In the absence of these experiences, men do not have an instinctual drive to nurture infants and children.
The civilizing effects of marriage	Because a man's contribution to reproduction is limited to the moment of conception, active and consistent parenting on the part of men is universally difficult to achieve. The best way to ensure that men will consistently provide for and nurture young children is to provide a social structure in which men can be assured of paternity (i.e., the traditional nuclear family). Without the social institution of marriage, men are likely to impregnate as many women as possible, without behaving responsibly toward their offspring.
The importance of a male role model	If men can be induced to take care of young children, their unique, masculine contribution significantly improves developmental outcomes for children. This is especially true for boys, who need a male role model to achieve a psychologically healthy masculine gender identity.

responsible, caretaking adult who has a positive emotional connection to them and with whom they have a consistent relationship. Because of the emotional and practical stress involved in child rearing, a family structure that includes more than one such adult is more likely to contribute to positive child outcomes. Neither the sex of the adult(s) nor the biological relationship to the child has emerged as a significant variable in predicting positive development. One, none, or both of those adults could be a father (or mother). We have found that the stability of the emotional connection and the predictability of the caretaking relationship are the significant variables that predict positive child adjustment.

···

Many social scientists believe that it is possible to draw a sharp distinction between scientific fact and political values. From our perspective, science is always structured by values, both in the research questions that are generated and in the interpretation of data. For example, if one considers the heterosexual nuclear family to be the optimal family structure for child development, then one is likely to design research that looks for negative consequences associated with growing up in a gay or lesbian parented family. If, in contrast, one assumes that gay and lesbian parents can create a positive family context, then one is likely to initiate research that investigates the strengths of children raised in these families.

···

We acknowledge that our reading of the scientific literature supports our political agenda. Our goal is to generate public policy initiatives that support men in their fathering role, without discriminating against women and same-sex couples. We are also interested in encouraging public policy that supports the legitimacy of diverse family structures, rather than policy that privileges the two-parent, heterosexual, married family.

···

Fathers Make a Unique and Essential Contribution to Child Development

The neoconservative perspective has proposed that if men can be induced to take care of young children, their unique, masculine contribution significantly improves the developmental outcomes for children. From the essentialist perspective, "fatherhood privileges children.... Conversely, the primary consequences of fatherlessness are rising male violence and declining child well-being and the underlying source of our most important social problems" (Blankenhorn, 1995, pp. 25–26).

These claims represent an oversimplification of the data. On average, children from divorced families have been shown to be at greater risk for a range of problems than are children from nondivorced families. However, it is also true that 75 percent of children from divorced families exhibit no negative effects (see Hetherington et al., 1998, for a review). Furthermore, the size of the negative effect of divorce is considerably reduced when the adjustment of children preceding divorce is controlled. For many of these children, the problems attributed to divorce were actually present prior to the divorce. In addition, divorce does not affect all children negatively. Amato, Loomis, and Booth (1995) reported that, although children from low-conflict marriages were stressed by divorce, the adjustment of children in high-conflict marriages actually improved after divorce. Overall, the research suggests that divorce does not irretrievably harm the majority of children.

...

Another major limitation to this paradigm is that father absence is not a monolithic variable. Qualitative research has shown that relationships between absent fathers and their children can vary widely. Weil (1996) studied 22 divorced fathers who were recruited from a self-help fathers' rights group. These middle-class, suburban, mostly white fathers used a variety of settings (e.g., school, day care, extended-family events) to increase their interaction with their children above the limited contact specified in their visitation arrangements. In another study, Way and Stauber (1996) interviewed 45 urban adolescent girls about their relationships with their fathers. Of the 26 girls who did not live with their fathers, 7 reported weekly contact with them, 10 reported occasional contact, and only 9 reported almost no contact. Thus, father involvement exists on a continuum, whether or not fathers live with their children. Fathers can be absent even when they reside with their children and can be present despite nonresident status.

The essentialist position also fails to acknowledge the potential costs of father presence. Engle and Breaux (1998) have shown that some fathers' consumption of family resources in terms of gambling, purchasing alcohol, cigarettes, or other nonessential commodities, actually increased women's workload and stress level.

The Importance of a Male Role Model

Another aspect of the neoconservative perspective is the argument that "key parental tasks belong essentially and primarily to fathers" (Blankenhorn, 1995, p. 67). Fathers are seen as essential role models for boys, relationship models for girls, and "protectors" of their families (Popenoe, 1996, p. 77). However, there is a considerable body of empirical evidence that contradicts these claims.

The essentialist perspective assumes that boys need a heterosexual male parent to establish a masculine gender identity. Pleck (1995) has demonstrated that empirical research does not support this assumption. Similarly, a significant amount of research on the children of lesbian and gay parents has shown that children raised by lesbian mothers (and gay fathers) are as likely as children raised in heterosexual, two-parent families to achieve a heterosexual gender orientation (Patterson, 1995; Patterson and Chan, 1997). Other aspects of personal development and social relationships were also found to be within the normal range for children raised in lesbian and gay families.

...

We speculate that the larger cultural context of male dominance and negative attitudes toward women may interfere with the ability of many single mothers to establish an authoritative parenting style with male children. Within patriarchal culture, boys know that when they become adult men, they will be dominant to every woman, including their mother. This cultural context, unmediated by a male presence, may undermine a single mother's authority with her sons. Qualitative research is needed to explore the subjective experiences of boys in single-mother, single-father, and two-parent nuclear families in order to understand these persistent but unclear findings.

Taken as a whole, the empirical research does not support the idea that fathers make a unique and essential contribution to child development. From our perspective, it is not the decline of marriage that is discouraging responsible fathering. Rather, various social conditions inhibit involved parenting by unmarried and divorced men.

...

Change and the Change-Back Reaction

If the essentialist paradigm is not supported by empirical data, why has it been so widely accepted? We believe that the appeal of the essentialist position reflects a reaction against the rapid changes in family life that have taken place in the past three decades....

In this context of rapid change, the neoconservative position reflects a widespread societal anxiety about who will raise the children. Mothers are no longer at home, and society has not embraced other-than-mother care. The United States, in contrast to other Western countries, has not yet developed a social policy agenda designed to help women and men integrate their work and family responsibilities. Thus, many people believe that a return to the traditional nuclear family structure with its gendered division of labor would be preferable to large numbers of neglected and unsupervised children.

In addition to an authentic concern about the welfare of children, we believe that the appeal of the essential father also reflects a backlash against the gay rights and feminist movements. In the past two decades, the employment of women has dramatically increased, whereas the employment of men has declined significantly (Engle and Breaux, 1998). Many more women than in past historical periods can now choose to leave unsatisfactory marriages or to have children on their own, outside of the context of a traditional marriage. Two of three divorces are now initiated by women (Rice, 1994).

Just as the feminist movement created new opportunities for women, the gay rights movement has encouraged many more gay men and lesbians to live an openly homosexual lifestyle. Many gay men and women who would previously have entered into a heterosexual marriage to have children, now see a gay family structure as a viable alternative for raising children. Parallel to these changes is the tendency emerging among heterosexual couples to live together and delay marriage until after a first pregnancy (Blossfeld, 1995). Thus, the distinctions between marital and cohabiting unions and between marital and nonmarital childbearing are losing their normative force.

These social changes require heterosexual men to relinquish certain aspects of power and privilege that they enjoyed in the context of the traditional nuclear family. Most men no longer have sole economic power over their families. Similarly, most men must accept some degree of responsibility for child care and household tasks. The majority of heterosexual men no longer have full-time wives to buffer the stress of balancing work and family roles. Within this new context of power sharing and role sharing, heterosexual men have been moved from the center to the margins of many versions of family life. In our view, the societal debate about gender differences in parenting is, in part, a reaction to this loss of male power and privilege. We see the argument that fathers are essential as an attempt to reinstate male dominance by restoring the dominance of the traditional nuclear family with its contrasting masculine and feminine gender roles.

...

From our perspective, the emphasis on the essential importance of fathers and heterosexual marriage represents a change-back reaction. It is an attempt to reassert the cultural hegemony of traditional values, such as heterocentrism, Judeo-Christian marriage, and male power and privilege.

Key Websites

THE NATIONAL FATHERS NETWORK (NFN)

This is a nonprofit organization that believes that men are crucially important in the lives of their families and children. They provide support and resources to fathers and families of children with developmental disabilities and chronic illness, and to the professionals who serve them. The NFN produces curriculum and training for health-care providers and educators, and a wealth of other innovative resources.
http://www.fathersnetwork.org/mn/index1.html

NATIONAL CENTER ON FATHERS AND FAMILIES

The mission of the National Center on Fathers and Families is to improve the life chances of children and the efficacy of families and to support the conduct and dissemination of research that advances the understanding of father involvement.
http://www.ncoff.gse.upenn.edu/mission.htm

SLOWLANE—STAY-AT-HOME DADS

This site serves as a resource, reference, and network for Stay-At-Home Dads (SAHD) and their families. The site provides dads with a searchable collection of articles and media clips written by, for, and about primary caregiving fathers. It also hosts multiple websites for at-home dads, including independent SAHD groups and several local dad-to-dad chapters, all of whose missions are to help dads connect with each other in their local areas. Slowlane boasts an extensive collection of links to sites for all fathering issues, including local and international dad organizations, single dads, new dads, divorced dads, custody issues, personal stories, and connecting with other dads.
http://www.slowlane.com

NATIONAL CENTER ON FATHERS AND FAMILIES: WORKING PAPERS

These working papers and monographs are intended to highlight critical and emerging topics in the field of fathers and their families. Monographs may take the form of papers by a single author, an edited volume of papers, or a list of recent books and papers along with book reviews by their research staff.
http://fatherfamilylink.gse.upenn.edu/org/ncoff/wrkppr/wrkppr.htm

THE FATHERHOOD PROJECT® HOME PAGE

James A. Levine, Ph.D., Director; Edward W. Pitt, M.S.W., Associate Director: The Fatherhood Project® is a national research and education project that is examining the future of fatherhood and developing ways to support men's involvement in child rearing. Its books, films, consultation services, seminars, and training programs all present practical strategies to support fathers and mothers in their parenting roles.
http://www.fatherhoodproject.org

AMERICAN COALITION FOR FATHERS AND CHILDREN

This is an organization dedicated to the creation of a family law system and legislative system that promotes equal rights for all parties affected by divorce, the breakup of a family, or the establishment of paternity. They believe that fathers through their involvement in their children's lives can have a positive effect on their emotional and psychological well-being. They believe that equal, shared parenting time or joint custody is the optimal custody situation. The site has links to an extensive list of articles and sites related to fatherhood issues.
http://www.acfc.org/html/study.htm

THE SOCIETY FOR THE PSYCHOLOGICAL STUDY OF MEN AND MASCULINITY

This is a division of the American Psychological Association founded in 1990. The society consists of men and women dedicated to promoting the critical study of how gender shapes and constricts men's lives, and it is committed to the enhancement of men's capacity to experience their full human potential.
http://web.indstate.edu/spsmm

Is the Widespread Use of Day Care Harming Our Children?

The need for child care is increasingly becoming a fact of life as more women stay in the work force after giving birth and as the number of single parents increases. In 1980, according to U.S. Census Bureau data, 38 percent of mothers ages 18 to 44 with infants under one year of age worked outside the home. By 1997 this figure had climbed to 54 percent. Most of these women return to work at some time during the child's first three to five months (National Institute of Child Health, 1997).

There are three types of child care for the children of working mothers. Approximately 32.8 percent of these children are cared for in their own homes—principally by their fathers or by members of the extended family. In the second type of arrangement, usually referred to as "family day care," a woman takes four to six unrelated young children into her home on a regular basis; 31.3 percent of child care is of this type. Another 29.3 percent of children are enrolled in day-care centers. An additional 5.5 percent are cared for by a parent (typically the mother) while they are working (U.S. Bureau of the Census, 1997).

With many parents putting their preschoolers in organized child care, many people ask how well this arrangement serves the children when compared with traditional child rearing. Sociologists begin to answer this question by noting that just as not all parenting is uniformly good, neither is all day care uniformly mediocre. High-quality day care does exist, and it can be a suitable substitute for home parenting. Unfortunately, poor-quality care, which threatens the child with serious physical and psychological harm, is also readily available.

High-quality day care is largely dependent on the adult-child ratio in the facility and on the overall group size in which children are cared for.

Staffing guidelines recommend that there be a child-care-worker-to-child ratio of 1:3 for infants under two; 1:4 for toddlers; and 1:7 for preschoolers. Unfortunately, many day care centers fall short in this area. The National Child Care Staffing Study found that the average adult-child ratio for infants was nearly 1:4, for toddlers 1:6, and for preschoolers 1:8. The average group size for infants was 7, for toddlers almost 10, and for preschoolers almost 14. Nearly half of all settings exceeded optimal guidelines (NCCSS; Whitebook, Phillips, and Howe, 1993).

Critics of day care have argued that sensitive and responsive caregiving is vital to developing a secure feeling of attachment between the parent and the child, and that long periods in day care threaten this connection. Responsive caregiving causes the child to be more successful with peers and in school, whereas children without this experience tend to be more aggressive and to misbehave in school.

Maggie Gallagher, in her article "Day Careless," cites research suggesting that children in full-time day care are less likely to be firmly attached to their parents and are on average more disobedient toward adults and more aggressive toward their peers than children cared for primarily by their parents.

Kristin Droege, in her article "Child Care: An Educational Perspective," notes that as day care has become a common reality for many children, it may be too simplistic to ask whether day care is good or bad in itself. What is really important is what the quality of the day care is. Studies show that children who spend time in high-quality child care are just as likely to have secure attachment relationships as are children who stay at home. In addition, quality child care can lead to better mother-child interaction (National Institutes of Health, 1997). Children whose home circumstances are less than ideal, but who attend high-quality day care, have been shown to benefit from the relationship they develop with a sensitive and responsive child-care provider.

Yes

Day Careless

Maggie
Gallagher

Until recently, parents typically had a far more negative view of day care than experts did. Not long ago, I stumbled across the following datum in a 1992 issue of the *Journal of the American Medical Association* that may help explain why: In the course of one year of full-time day care, a middle-class white male toddler was "likely to be bitten" *nine times.*

A social scientist might point out that there is no firm evidence that being mauled by one's peers has any negative effect on one's psychosocial development. But I have never run across the parent who, faced with this bit of news, does not shudder. That is the difference between a social scientist and a parent.

But over the last decade, the gap between expert and folk wisdom appears to be closing. A growing number of child-development experts have joined the ranks of parents who worry that extensive day care is not good for young children.

An emerging body of research suggests that children in full-time day care are less likely to be firmly attached to their parents and are on average more disobedient toward adults and more aggressive toward their peers than children cared for primarily by their parents. In certain circumstances, day care also puts children's cognitive development at risk.

Of course, not all children in day care are damaged by the experience. But the new data should give parents—and policymakers—pause....

A review of the day-care literature was published in 1996 by Michael E. Lamb of the National Institute of Child Health and Human Development

(NICHHD). While noting that nonparental care "need not" have harmful effects, Lamb concluded that it often does, depending "on the quality of care and the child's age, temperament, and individual background." Under ideal circumstances—when the child develops a strong, stable attachment to an alternative caregiver—day care may not be harmful. But, he concludes, "in other circumstances, [nonparental care] leads to behavior problems (including aggression and noncompliance)."

The trouble is that most day-care kids are, indeed, in "other circumstances." Quality child care, as experts now understand it, does not refer to variables such as group size or caregiver training that can be regulated by government (day-care boosters tend to be obsessed with licensing and training). Instead, quality care is dependent on the same underlying emotional processes that make for strong mother-child relationships. For young children, high-quality care means a caregiver who stays with the child for long periods—"years, not months," says one expert. A high-quality caregiver babbles, chatters, coos, hugs, strokes a baby or toddler, and consistently makes the effort to respond warmly to his verbal and nonverbal attempts at communication.

Few employees can meet such demanding standards. A 1995 national study by the University of Colorado found that only 8 percent of day-care centers serving infants and toddlers offer high-quality care; in 40 percent of centers, the care is so bad that it endangers young children's psychological and cognitive development. Indeed, for cognitive development, the research suggests that the children of educated mothers may be at special risk—because of the contrast between the care they get at home and at the typical day-care center.

Just how harmful is the day care most children receive? The evidence falls into two categories. The first comes from medical researchers. Day care, it turns out, is definitely not good for babies' health. This is not surprising: Group care exposes babies and toddlers to large numbers of biological strangers, many of whom are not toilet trained and who drool, making day care a breeding ground for infectious disease.

...

Overall, according to a 1989 estimate by Dr. Haskins in the *Bulletin of the New York Academy of Medicine*, the excess illness attributable to day care costs American families and society $1.8 billion and the lives of at least 100 children each year.

The medical consequences of group care should be disturbing enough. But nearly as chilling is the large number of studies that link early, extensive day care with psychological, social, and behavioral problems.

A 1994 international meta-analysis by Claudio Violato and Clare Russell of the University of Calgary, involving over 22,000 children, concludes: "Full-time care for infants and young children [puts] a substantial proportion of the population at risk for psychological maladaptation."

Almost 50 percent of day-care children, for example, had an insecure attachment to their mothers, compared to about 30 percent in the population as a whole.

...

Sons of mothers who worked more than 35 hours a week were also less likely to be securely attached to their fathers. As a result, almost 30 percent of day-care kids were insecurely attached to both parents, compared to just 7 percent of children in families that used less than 20 hours a week of nonparental care.

Many (though not all) studies also find that children in extensive day care are more aggressive with peers and less compliant with the requests of adults.... Day-care kids also received lower academic and conduct grades and were rated more difficult to discipline....

And in 1991 Jay Belsky and David Eggebeen studied a large national sample in the *National Longitudinal Survey on Youth*. They found that four-to-six-year-old children were much more likely to be rated "less compliant" if, during their first two years of life, their mothers had worked more than 30 hours a week. Again, early and extensive day care had more influence on a child's behavior than family characteristics such as socioeconomic status or the mother's education.

Michael Lamb, in his review of day-care literature for the NICHHD, found these tendencies turning up over and over again, "particularly when the care is of poorer quality."

Day-care defenders faced with such dark data show an almost comic insistence on looking at the bright side of life. "Children who have been in day care," suggests Alison Clarke Stewart, in a 1989 article for *The American Psychologist*, "think for themselves" and "want their own way." Striking a blow for infant independence everywhere, "They are not willing to comply with adults' arbitrary rules...."

When redefining childhood virtue does not suffice, day-care defenders are apt to resort to the "per se" defense. There is no evidence that day care "per se" is harmful to children; after all, many children in day care do just fine. What harms children, they argue, is low-quality care.

The NICHHD's ongoing highly publicized seven-year day-care study is perhaps the biggest, most sophisticated attempt to disentangle the effects of quality of day care from the effects of quantity of day care. This study is using a diverse but not a nationally representative sample, with the parents being predominantly white, married, and middle class. The results have been widely trumpeted as offering a clean bill of health for day care. The reality is more complex. The first report, released last year, analyzed infants' attachment to their mothers at 15 months. The study found a pattern of dual risks for infants in day care: In the case of mothers who were relatively less sensitive to their children's needs, placement in as little as 10 hours of day care each week regardless of quality, or in low-quality care, or with more than one caregiver in the first year, made it more likely that those children would be insecurely attached to their mothers.

Jay Belsky, a professor at Penn State University and one of many researchers involved in the design and analysis of the NICHHD study, points out that this study may understate the dangers of day care for the average family. "The most stressed, least sensitive mothers," he says, "are the group that looks most vulnerable, and they are also least represented in the NICHHD sample—we may have underestimated the effects of day care."

The second batch of analyses, reported last spring, also contained some disturbing results from direct observations of mother-child relations. "What we found was an intriguing, consistent, and disconcerting pattern people run away from," Belsky notes: More time in day care led to a small, but measurable, deterioration in mother-child relationships.

The deterioration was evident both in terms of mothers' attitudes toward their children and in terms of children's attitudes toward their mothers. More time in day care was related to less-sensitive mothering when the child was 6 months, more negative maternal interactions when the child was 15 months, and an increase in insensitive mothering at 36 months. Meanwhile, day-care children were less positively oriented toward and engaged with their mothers, and expressed less affection for them at age three.

Although the magnitude of these changes is not large, as Professor Belsky points out, the direction of the changes is clear and consistent: Children who spend more time in day care develop weaker and more problematic relationships with their mothers.

Put the NICHHD findings together, and the pattern becomes even more disturbing. Day care has the worst immediate effects on children with less-sensitive mothers. And, over time, women who put their children into day care become somewhat less sensitive.

...

In the NICHHD sample, the amount of time a child spent in day care had in itself no effect on cognitive development, but quality of care did. Again, quality of care, in this context, refers not to externals but to how much caregivers talk to their charges. Given the research on the quality of existing infant care, the NICHHD study thus strongly suggests that most children now placed in early day care are at intellectual risk. This is particularly true when educated mothers leave their babies in the care of less-educated caregivers.

...

Even older children may suffer when mothers work long hours and leave them with others. Several recent studies suggest, in the words of sociologists Paul Amato and Alan Booth, that "mothers who work part-time have more academically competent children, on average, than do mothers who work long hours or who are not in the labor force." Mothers who work part-time, for example, are more likely than those employed full-time to discuss school with children, check their homework, and restrict their television viewing.

...

As troubling as the immediate effects of day care on children are questions about the long-term effects of day care on families. Will people who, as children, spent most of their waking hours cared for by employees still feel obliged to help care for ailing parents in their old age? Will they place as high a value on family life? Is it likely that the two-career day-care model is contributing to the decline of marriage and family life? Research to date provides no definitive answers, but some disturbing clues.

Several researchers, for example, have found that very young children whose mothers work full-time tend to have poorer relations not only with their mothers but also with their fathers....

Weakened attachment of fathers to children may, in turn, help explain the fact that marriages in which both partners work full-time are far more prone to divorce. Even when two-career couples stay together, their children may not. According to research by Amato and Booth, women whose mothers worked full-time are 166 percent more likely to end up divorced, even after taking into account the parents' marital status and the daughters' own education and career achievements.

The data confirm common sense: Attitudes matter. Family-centered parents tend to raise family-centered children, who value stable marriage in no small part because it permits children to be cared for by their own kin.

One of the long-standing findings of day-care research is that children suffer both when mothers who want to work stay at home, and when mothers who would prefer to stay at home must work. But, in the real world, mothers who want to put their babies into day care are a rare breed. Researchers in one small study who tried to distinguish between the effects of maternal satisfaction and those of day care found that the data did not permit them to do so: because, to their surprise, "the dissatisfied mothers were predominantly the employed mothers and the satisfied mothers the nonemployed (and largely the part-time employed as well)," note Margaret Owen and Martha J. Cox.

...

Thus, it stands to reason, the more that outside pressures—including government subsidies—help push grudging parents into using day care, the worse the negative effects of day care are likely to become.

...

Whether the current research raises big warning flags or small ones depends in part on how unusual the modern form of commercial day care is as a child-rearing method. Day-care advocates like to portray exclusive parental care of children as a historical anomaly. "They say mothers have always shared caregiving," Belsky remarks. "That passes off as intellectual sophistication these days. What they don't go on to say is that in aboriginal societies where mothers share caregiving they do so with networks of blood relatives—with people who will know both the parents and the child their whole lives." By contrast, the current reality of day care—children cared for by a series of biological strangers who have no long-term commitment to the child or the parents—is an experiment unprecedented in human history.

Parents, of course, instinctively know this. One of the best-kept secrets in the child-care debate is that most parents, including a majority of working mothers, try hard to keep child care in the family.

...

American families' strong, demonstrated preference for care by kin is consistent with the practices of every other human society that has ever existed and with the growing data on the effect of day care on children. In a January 1997 NBC/*Wall Street Journal* poll, Americans were asked to name the two or three most important issues facing the nation "that you personally would like to see the federal government in Washington do something about." Just 1 percent said child care.

The day-care debate is often portrayed as pitting old-fashioned stay-at-home moms against the needs of modern working women. But the reality is that almost half of mothers of young children who work are not in the market for child care at all....

So who benefits from subsidized day care? There is one obvious answer: the day-care industry, a multibillion-dollar concern which, like so many businesses, looks to use the power of government to increase its profits. To promote government subsidies only for those who use commercial child care is to push a service that is actively harmful for some children and one that most parents emphatically do not want. In other words, it is the kind of social policy only Washington could love.

Child Care:
An Educational Perspective

Kristin Droege

What Is Meant by "Child Care"?

The term *child care* is used to refer to any form of care for children that is not provided by parents. Child-care centers, the most familiar form, exist in many churches, synagogues, and community centers, and have in the last 10 years appeared both in the parents' workplaces (in the form of corporate-sponsored programs) and in the for-profit sector. Family day-care homes, in which a woman provides child care in her own home, are also a very popular style of child care. Other arrangements include in-home nannies and au pairs; independent preschool and nursery school programs; early-childhood programs established through universities and private or parochial schools; and having children stay with a friend, neighbor, or relative for regular and consistent periods of time throughout the week.

Child care is not new to American culture (Clarke-Stewart, 1982). The first day nurseries were established in the mid-1800s when the Industrial Revolution brought women out of the homes and into the factories. During the Great Depression, public funds were first applied toward child care as an attempt to provide work for unemployed teachers, nurses, cooks, and janitors. Then came World War II. With women working in the factories, child care boomed. By 1945 over 1.5 million children attended child care. When the war ended, so did the boom. In the mid-sixties, with the women's movement, preschool programs and early-childhood education began growing in popularity again. At this time, early childhood

From *Jobs and Capital* 9 (winter 1995). Copyright © 1995. Reprinted with the permission of the Milken Institute for Job and Capital Formation.

also became the focus of increased attention from researchers in the fields of psychology and education. Today, early-childhood education and child care are almost indistinguishable. Almost every care arrangement for children under the age of six claims to provide the child with an environment and activities that will assist the child's growth physically, intellectually, socially, and emotionally. Parents and educators now commonly expect that child care is meant to serve the needs of working parents while simultaneously benefiting the development of the child.

Child Care and Child Development

What do we actually know about children's needs throughout the preschool years and the impact of full-time child-care arrangements on their development? Research has analyzed several areas of development in relation to children's child-care experiences (Scarr, 1989). The earliest research focused on children's attachment relationships, examining the possibility that separation from the mother, especially during infancy, could damage the mother-child relationship believed to be so influential on later social development and competency. Research later shifted to include more direct study of the impact of child care on social development. Social development throughout childhood plays a crucial role in preparing the child to function successfully in society. The mother-child attachment relationship and later social skills developed with adults and peers predict the individual's ability to maintain friendships, working relationships, intimate relationships, and parental relationships in later adult life.

Attachment

Attachment theory has gained enormous popularity in the field of developmental psychology over the past 10 years. Based on the work of John Bowlby, attachment theory asserts that children, predominantly through their interactions and experiences with their mother during the first year of life, develop an internal working model of their own value as a human being and the role of "others" in their life (Bretherton, 1985). Simply stated, if a child receives sensitive and responsive caregiving in the first year of life, attachment theory predicts that the child will develop a working model of himself as worthy of love. He also develops a view of "others" as generally trustworthy and good. A sensitive and responsive caregiver consistently and appropriately responds to the child's social bids, or requests, and initiates interactions that are geared to the child's capacities, intentions, moods, goals, and developmental level (Howes, 1989). The child's internal working model, or view of the role and importance of self and others, would result in a secure attachment relationship with the mother.

On the other hand, a child whose mother is insensitive to her needs, unresponsive to her bids, or, in the extreme case, abusive or neglectful, is expected to develop an insecure attachment relationship with her mother. The insecure relationship is the result of an internal working model of the child as unworthy of love and of "others" as insensitive or untrustworthy. It is believed that the internal working model that is developed in infancy serves as a basis for the child's approach to social interactions and relationships throughout life.

...

As the body of research on the subject grew, however, it became clear that the effects of child care were not so clear-cut. Two further waves of research resulted (Howes and Hamilton, 1991). While the first wave of researchers was still arguing over whether or not child care was good for children's development, the second wave began examining the differences in the care provided to children who had secure versus insecure attachment relationships. How does the kind of child care provided influence child development and, specifically, attachment? Researchers found easily identifiable markers of care that produced positive versus negative developmental outcomes in children. These markers, which will be discussed in detail later, came to be identified as indicators of high-quality child care. Children who spent time in high-quality child care were just as likely to have secure attachment relationships with their mothers as children who stayed at home. It was also discovered that children who had insecure attachment relationships with their mothers, but who attended high-quality child care, were capable of forming secure attachment relationships with their child-care providers. A sensitive and responsive child-care provider may compensate for a mother-child relationship that is insecure. The picture was, therefore, not so grim when the quality of the child-care arrangement was considered.

Social Development

Researchers have continued to explore the impact on children's social development of high-quality child care and greater exposure to a large peer group during infancy and the preschool years. Not only do we know that children who receive high-quality care appear more socially competent with peers than those in low-quality care (Howes and Olenick, 1987; Howes and Stewart, 1988); the research indicates that high-quality child care may, in fact, provide benefits to children that they do not receive in the typical home setting. The social importance of the early-childhood peer group was elaborated by Rubenstein and

Howes (1983), who suggested that children in child care with peers use their peers as a source of social support to assist with the separation from mother. Further, their work suggested that play with peers who have comparable cognitive and motor skills facilitates common interests and pleasures and allows previously acquired skills to be elaborated and elevated to more complex levels. For instance, a toddler may be able to roll the ball down the slide, but with a peer the game encourages a "give and take" situation with turns, in which one child rolls the ball down and the other pushes it back up. This expands the child's skills and abilities in both the social and cognitive realm. While the same interaction might take place with an adult a few times, it truly takes a peer to enjoy enacting this procedure 20 or 30 times in a row for several days on end until it is no longer novel and exciting

Further research has indicated many benefits for children in high-quality child-care arrangements. Children with child-care experience appear less timid and fearful, more outgoing, helpful, and cooperative with unfamiliar peers than children without child-care experience (Clarke-Stewart, 1982). Children who have experience with a stable group of peers demonstrate social play skills that are more complex and reciprocal than those whose peer group has been unstable due to frequent changes in child-care arrangements (Howes and Stewart, 1988). Children who have experienced a stable peer group are more likely to function successfully in the social relationships they will experience in later childhood and adulthood, such as those encountered in school, work, and family settings.

...

One of the most common options parents choose for the care of their young children is the use of relatives. Approximately 20 percent of all working mothers place their young child in the care of relatives, either in their own home or in the home of a relative (Galinsky, Howes, Kontos, and Shinn, 1994). However, the Study of Children in Family Child Care and Relative Care (Galinsky et al., 1994) found that 69 percent of all of the relative care examined proved to be inadequate care, in terms of the quality issues raised earlier. Relative care received lower quality ratings than licensed family day-care homes. While many parents feel it is safest and most convenient to leave their child with a family member, licensed family day-care providers were more likely to plan activities for the children, and had more training in the field than did the relatives.

This is not to say that the nonprofit market has not responded at all to the increased demand for child-care spaces. More child-care centers and family day-care homes exist today than ever before and they continue to open at high rates. So some might say that the real problems are short-term and that the market will respond to provide the necessary number of care facilities. However, there are a few problems with that scenario, and they revolve around the issues of quality that I have discussed.

The first problem is one of information. Some families who can afford the price of high-quality care choose lower-quality care because they lack information about the benefits of high-quality care, what high-quality care looks like, and how to find it. A distressing obstacle to high-quality child care is the centers' ability to disguise the quality of their care. Many parents visit and inspect the child-care center that they intend to use for their child. The information that is conveyed by a 20-minute visual inspection of a child-care center can, however, be misleading and deceptive.

...

One solution is to educate parents about the importance of a high-quality child development program, what high quality means, and how to identify it. Government investment in the creation and dissemination of information about early-childhood education would be a public service that could benefit the larger community. Better information could educate parents about the importance of such issues as turnover rates and educational backgrounds of caregivers, and assist parents in asking the questions necessary to elicit such information.

The next problem is the loss of social benefits. Society has an interest in children being prepared to enter school. Yet many parents choose not to use high-quality care because of considerations other than the quality of the child development program. When parents make the decision to enroll their child in child care they must weigh many factors into the equation. Most parents probably consider the first priority to be a program that keeps their child safe, healthy, and happy. But simultaneously they take into account the convenience of the center's location, the hours that the center remains open, its policy for sick children and late pick-ups, and, most important, the fees that the center charges. When parents choose a center they often trade off their standards concerning the quality of its child development program in exchange for their logistical needs or their budget.

Thus, if people buy only the child care they are willing or able to pay for, they tend to buy lower-quality care than is optimal for the larger society. An additional investment, however, which could provide a higher-quality child development program, extended hours, or a broader sick-child care program, would benefit the larger community as well as the individual family and child. For the community, for example, this investment could yield children attending the local public schools who are more socially skilled, cognitively advanced, with more advanced communication skills, and thus more likely to succeed academically.

Since this additional investment in child care yields benefits to the larger community, it merits our attention to find additional sources of funding. Although some oppose government investment in child care, they have in fact always contributed to the expense of caring for the young children in our country through the lost tax revenues of women who worked in their homes raising their children. Government investment in quality child-care programs can yield social benefits to children, families, and the broader community.

Key Websites

THE FAMILIES AND WORK INSTITUTE

The mission of this group is to provide data to help with decisions regarding work and family issues. It provides research on a variety of studies including day-care issues, parenting issues, and workplace issues.
http://www.familiesandwork.org

BEHIND THE PUSH FOR DAY CARE ...
PARENTS AT HOME: STILL THE SILENT MAJORITY

Charmaine Crouse Yoest, *Behind the Push for Day Care ... Parents at Home: Still the Silent Majority*: In January 1998, President Clinton and first lady Hillary Rodham Clinton announced a historic initiative: $20 billion in increased federal spending for child care over the next five years. This, they said, would address a silent child-care crisis afflicting the nation. This paper examines the underlying assumptions and common perceptions used to buttress such an expansion of federal involvement in day care. It asks whether there is a crisis in America today over child care. If so, it asks, is day care the answer?
http://www.frc.org/fampol/fp98ccc.html

A SOCIOLOGICAL PERSPECTIVE ON CHILD-CARE RESEARCH

Until recently, sociologists have paid far less attention to child-care issues than to other aspects of family life. This paper examines child-care research from a sociological perspective. The themes include the demand for and availability of child-care services, strategies for managing work-family conflicts, the division of labor within families, and child-care policy issues.
http://www.childcarecanada.org/resources/CRRUpubs/op2/2op6.html

THE NATIONAL CHILD CARE INFORMATION CENTER

The National Child Care Information Center, established by the U.S. Department of Health and Human Services, seeks to serve as a mechanism for supporting quality, comprehensive services for children and families.
http://www.nccic.org

TALKING TO CHILDREN: THE EFFECTS OF THE HOME
AND THE FAMILY DAY CARE ENVIRONMENT

This study was designed to provide information about the nature of home and family day-care environments and how those environments affect a child's language development. Children's environments at home and in

family day care were rated for their level of cognitive stimulation on the *HOME* scale, and mother-child and caregiver-child discourse patterns were analyzed for evidence of developmentally facilitative discourse features.
http://www.childcarecanada.org/resources/CRRUpubs/op2/2op10.html

SHORT-TERM AND LONG-TERM EFFECTS OF EARLY PARENTAL EMPLOYMENT ON CHILDREN OF THE NATIONAL LONGITUDINAL SURVEY OF YOUTH

Elizabeth Harvey, "Short-Term and Long-Term Effects of Early Parental Employment on Children of the National Longitudinal Survey of Youth," *Developmental Psychology* 35, no. 2 (March 1999): This study examined the effects of early parental employment on children in the National Longitudinal Survey of Youth. Minimal effects on children's later functioning were found. Early maternal employment was not consistently related to children's development. Early parental employment appeared to be somewhat more beneficial for single mothers and lower-income families.
http://www.apa.org/journals/dev/dev352445.html

THE EUROPEAN NETWORK "FAMILY & WORK"

This network attempts to disseminate and exchange innovative practices in reconciling work and family issues. The site focuses on new forms of work organization, working-hour flexibility, and professional mobility.
http://europa.eu.int/comm/dg05/family-net

THE NATIONAL SURVEY OF THE CHANGING WORKFORCE

James T. Bond and Ellen Galinsky, "The National Survey of the Changing Workforce": The researchers in this study used a nationally representative sample of the U.S. labor force and compared it with a 1977 sample to provide a 20-year perspective on the changing work force.
http://www.familiesandwork.org/summary/nscw.pdf

Is Today's High Divorce Rate a Problem for Society?

Throughout most of history, marriage was considered a permanent pairing of two people, and divorce was a rare phenomenon. Under English law, the most a couple wishing to live apart from each other could hope for was a church-sanctioned divorce known as a *mensa et thoro*, which was not an actual divorce but a "separation from bed and board."

Part of the reason for such a low divorce rate was that marriage, for both men and women, was primarily an economic partnership—a way to pool labor and resources in order to survive. The presence or absence of romantic love was not an important factor in the marriage. Having food on the table and a place to live were the most important factors.

Divorce continued to be rare until the 1940s, when large numbers of women entered the work force. This produced changes in women's economic potential and also increased social interaction between male and female coworkers. An increase in divorces followed. Many of these divorces were obtained by fraud and collusion between the spouses because there were very few grounds for divorce.

No-fault divorce was first introduced in California in 1969. Previously, only adultery had been recognized as grounds for divorce in that state. A divorce could now be granted based on the "irretrievable breakdown of the marriage," which not only eliminated the showing of grounds for divorce but, as a practical matter, made it possible for one spouse to decide to divorce unilaterally without the consent of the other. Although one partner could conceivably contest a no-fault divorce, such a challenge rarely succeeded. Generally, the court granted the application because it was difficult to challenge a spouse's allegation that the marriage was irretrievably broken.

By 1985 all states, with the exception of New York, had virtually unrestricted no-fault divorce available to any married person who wanted one. The only restriction in most cases was a waiting period that could be as short as a few months and was rarely more than a year.

Today, 50 percent of all marriages end in divorce. Is this high divorce rate a problem for society? William A. Galston, in his essay "Divorce American Style," contends that it is. He points out that three-fifths of all divorces involve young children, causing 1 million children to be affected by divorce each year. The vast majority of these children end up in mother-only households, and many rarely see their fathers.

Galston notes that divorce has a negative effect on the well-being of children that shows itself in poorer school performance, lower high school completion and college attendance rates, higher rates of depression and other psychological illnesses, higher crime rates, more suicides, more out-of-wedlock births, and a greater likelihood that they will become divorced themselves.

Margaret Talbot, in her article "Love, American Style: What the Alarmists about Divorce Don't Get about Idealism in America," agrees that divorce has serious consequences, pushing families into poverty and psychologically wounding the children. Yet, she sees divorce as an expression of idealism about marriage. In a nation founded on the idea that it is better to dissolve a difficult marriage than to attempt to keep it together against all odds, divorce is an expression of our freedom. Having made a mistake in one marriage, we have the freedom to establish a more harmonious one, "a marriage that would neither be corrupted by adultery nor corroded by lovelessness."

Yes

Divorce American Style

William A.
Galston

...

The no-fault divorce revolution of the past quarter century was not in any simple sense the product of a male conspiracy. Many women's groups, lawyers, judges, academics, and family-practice professionals strongly favored this change, on the ground that it was needed to end (as one supporter put it) "the hypocrisy of strict divorce laws administered by a lenient process." And public opinion began swinging toward more relaxed laws in the mid-1960s.

The benefits of no-fault divorce were immediate, especially for men seeking an easier exit from long-established marriages. An understanding of the costs emerged more slowly, through painful experience and the gradual accretion of research. The principal victims have been women in long-established marriages, along with minor children. There has also been a broader casualty: the idea of marriage as a presumptively permanent relationship—as a structure of incentives for individuals to contribute to the well-being of the family, and a framework of reasonable expectations of reciprocal benefits over the lifetime of the partnership. And pervasive divorce has imposed large costs on society as a whole. For example, children's postdivorce psychological and behavioral problems have multiplied the challenges facing teaching, and jurisdictions at every level of the federal system have had to invest huge sums in child-support enforcement.

...

From *The Public Interest*, no. 124 (summer 1996). Copyright © 1996 by National Affairs, Inc. Reprinted with the permission of the author and *The Public Interest*.

The Casualties of Divorce

We have good reason to be worried about the current state of marriage and divorce in America. To be sure, the rate of divorce has been trending upward fitfully for more than a century. Still, the rate of divorce in 1960 was no higher than it had been in 1940, and not much higher than in 1920. (There was a spike right after World War II, but it quickly subsided.) Then, between 1960 and 1980, the rate of divorce surged by nearly 250 percent. Since then, it has stabilized, but at a rate that is the highest by far in the industrialized world. About half of all marriages undertaken today are likely to end in divorce. Forty percent of all first marriages will suffer that fate, compared to only 16 percent in 1960. Upwards of 60 percent of all remarriages will not endure.

Three-fifths of all divorces involve minor children. The number of children directly touched by divorce each year has doubled, from 485,000 in 1966 to about 1 million today. The percentage of children living in mother-only households (headed by never-married as well as divorced women) has also more than doubled. About 40 percent of children living in such households have not seen their fathers during the past year; only one in six sees them more than once a week.

Children typically encounter difficulties in the wake of divorce. The conventional wisdom is that these negative effects are attributable to two factors that are distinguishable from divorce itself: steep income losses after divorce and intrafamily conflicts before divorce. This is not entirely wrong: Predivorce conflict accounts for about half the observed postdivorce difficulties for boys and somewhat less than half for girls. And economic decline accounts for about half the remaining damage.

But the conventional wisdom of the 1970s and 1980s is not the whole truth. Since 1990, a number of leading researchers—Frank Furstenberg, Andrew Cherlin, Sara McLanahan, Gary Sandefur, and Nicholas Zill, among others—have assembled large quantities of original data and subjected it to rigorous analysis. Here is the consensus of their findings: There is a critical distinction between divorces involving physical abuse or extreme emotional cruelty and those that do not. Minor children in the former category are on balance better off than those whose parents had remained married. But the opposite is the case for the children in the latter category, where divorce follows lower-intensity conflict. Correcting for the effects of both income loss and predivorce conflict between parents, divorce in these cases has an independent, negative effect on the well-being of minor children along a number of key dimensions: school performance, high school completion, college attendance and graduation, labor-force attachment and work patterns, depression and other psychological illnesses, crime, suicide, out-of-wedlock births, and the propensity to become divorced.

...

Here's how Furstenberg and Cherlin summarize the implications of this emerging understanding:

> It is probably true that most children who live in a household filled with continual conflict between angry, embittered spouses would be better off if their parents split up—assuming that the level of conflict is lowered by the separation. And there is no doubt that the rise in divorce has liberated some children (and their custodial parents) from families marked by physical abuse, alcoholism, drugs, and violence. But we doubt that such clearly pathological descriptions apply to most families that disrupt. Rather, we think there are many more cases in which there is little open conflict, but one or both partners finds the marriage personally unsatisfying.... A generation ago, when marriage was thought of as a moral and social obligation, most husbands and wives in families such as this stayed together. Today, when marriage is thought of increasingly as a means of achieving personal fulfillment, many more will divorce. Under these circumstances, divorce may well make one or both spouses happier; but we strongly doubt that it improves the psychological well-being of the children.

Law, Economics, and Culture

What caused the explosion in the rate of divorce over the past 30 years is much debated. Economics may have played a role: Women surged into the paid work force in unprecedented numbers. Male salaries and wages declined, both absolutely and relative to those of women.

It was also a period of profound cultural change. Daniel Yankelovich has recently charted some of the key shifts. Compared to 30 years ago, Americans today place less value on obligation to others, on sacrifice, and on self-restraint. By contrast, we place more value on individualism, on self-expression and self-realization, and on personal choice.

These shifts are correlated with important changes in attitudes toward children, families, and marriage. Americans are far more accepting of divorce today than 30 years ago. We are far more likely to say that marriage is first and foremost a means to personal happiness. And we are far less inclined to believe that parents in a less than fully satisfactory marriage ought to make an effort to stay together for the sake of their children. Up to the mid-1960s, about half of all Americans thought that parents had an obligation to make this effort. By 1994, that figure had declined to about 20 percent.

But this period of rapid economic and cultural change has been accompanied by a period of rapid change in the law of divorce. As recently as 30 years ago, every state had a fault-based system. The standard grounds for divorce included adultery, physical abuse, mental cruelty, desertion, imprisonment, alcohol or drug addiction, and insanity. Within five years of the passage of California's 1969 no-fault statute, 45 states had followed suit. By 1985, the last bastions had crumbled; every state had either replaced its old fault system or had added important no-fault options.

It is tempting to conclude that the movement toward no-fault divorce is the product of the economic and cultural changes, and that it has had no independent effect on divorce rates or outcomes. This view was largely unchallenged until about a decade ago. But the tide is turning. While full scholarly returns are not yet in, evidence is accumulating that once instituted, no-fault laws further accelerated the pace of divorce. A 50-state survey published in the *Journal of Marriage and the Family* concluded that "the switch from fault divorce law to no-fault divorce law led to a measurable increase in the divorce rate."

...

And finally, there is the "destigmatization effect." There is no question that no-fault divorce laws symbolized the spreading belief that divorce presented no particular moral problem, that there was, in the moral as well as legal sense, no fault. As Harvard law professor Mary Ann Glendon has observed, in moving away from the legal standard of fault, we also set aside the moral standard of responsibility.

...

It Takes a Family

Families are composed of individuals with interests that converge only in part. We should divest ourselves of the romantic conception of perfect harmony, in which arrangements that serve the interests of husbands equally serve the interests of wives or of children. What is good for men who have worked outside the home all their adult lives may not be good for those women who have never done so. What is good for one or both parents may not be so good for minor children. And what may seem desirable for some families may have negative consequences for society as a whole.

The question before us is how best to deal with these tensions. During the past generation, we have encouraged, or at least tolerated, the development of a divorce law that has favored adults over children, and economically advantaged workers (usually male) over dependent spouses (usually female). The time has come to redress the balance, in a manner that requires individuals to assume greater responsibility for the interpersonal and social costs of their actions.

In the current cultural context, it is hard to make a case for restricting personal choice when the consequences of that choice affect only independent adults who are capable of asserting and defending their own interests. I am thinking in particular of marriages in which both spouses work and there are no children. Yet there is still a strong case to be made that the law should protect vulnerable individuals and the general interests of society.

Within this framework, I would propose three goals: First, we should endeavor to reduce the number of divorces, particularly, but not exclusively, those involving minor children. Second, when such divorces are unavoidable, we should seek divorces to mitigate the consequences for children. Third, we should restore a level playing field—and adequate protections—for women who choose the role of full-time mother.

Points of Intervention

There are three points at which we can intervene to reduce the incidence of divorce. The first occurs at or before the threshold of marriage. It is stunning how much time public education spends on sex while failing to discuss marriage in any sustained manner. It is a legitimate function of public education to treat marriage seriously as a human and social institution. Religious institutions have a role to play here too. For the overwhelming majority of Americans, marriage remains a sacrament and still takes place under the aegis of religion. If every church and synagogue took as one of its principal tasks the thorough preparation of young people for marriage, it could make a significant difference. There is some evidence that this strategy works best when all the religious institutions within a community unite around this objective in a mutually reinforcing way.

These educational efforts should be reinforced by the law. In most states it is much harder to get a driver's license than a marriage license. At a minimum, each state should impose a reasonable waiting period (at least one month, but preferably three) and require couples to show that they have completed a program of counseling (religious or secular) preparing them for marriage.

The second point of intervention occurs during marriage. At a minimum, we should systematically reexamine our economic and social policies (and our tax code) with an eye to building a marriage-friendly environment. The private sector can contribute as well, through flextime, telecommuting, job-sharing, part-time work with better benefits, and generous leave policies for family emergencies. Religious institutions should offer programs for couples who want to renew their marriages or to confront problems that could lead to marital dissolution if left unaddressed.

The third key point of intervention occurs at the threshold of divorce: We should change the current no-fault regime. As many observers have noted, the American law of divorce lurched from one extreme, where fault had to be demonstrated in nearly all cases, to the other extreme, where in most states either spouse can terminate the marriage without the other's consent. The sensible, moderate alternative—no-fault-divorce by mutual consent—was all but ignored. Only two states (New York and Mississippi) require mutual consent. In 40 states, divorce may be obtained after a separation of one year or less, regardless of the other spouse's opposition.

...

And states should certainly eliminate unilateral no-fault divorce for couples with minor children—and return to an updated fault system (one that, for example, takes into account what we've learned over the past two decades about spouse abuse). As an alternative to fault in unilateral cases, states could establish a five-year waiting period before a nonconsensual no-fault divorce is allowed to occur. Even in cases where both parties consent, there should be suitable braking mechanisms: a mandatory pause of at least a year for reflection, counseling, and mediation.

...

Save the Children

Even if divorce involving minor children cannot be prevented, there are steps we can take to mitigate the consequences. We have learned a great deal in the past decade about why divorce hurts children. I rely especially on the recent work of McLanahan and Sandefur, which identifies three principal causes of harm:

- Diminished income—roughly a 30 percent drop for children and the custodial parent
- Diminished parenting time from the noncustodial parent (usually the father) who detaches himself from his children and from the custodial parent (usually the mother) who has to combine work inside and outside the home
- Disruption of established ties—to friends, neighborhoods and communities, and educational institutions

With regard to the economics of divorce, I believe (following Mary Ann Glendon) that we should adopt a "children first" principle. Issues of property division should not even be discussed until adequate provision is made for the economic needs of children. When children opt for postsecondary education and training, child support should cover a reasonable share, at least until age 21. In addition, we need to get far more serious about child-support enforcement. Important legislation has been adopted in the past decade to enhance the capacity of states to work cooperatively, but we can and must go farther.

...

Fairness for Women in Long-Term Marriages

In addition to safeguarding the interests of children of divorce, we should also be mindful of the interests of a certain category of women. As I noted earlier, no-fault divorce especially harmed women in long-term marriages. This is, of course, morally unacceptable. In short, the law should not penalize women who have chosen to spend much of their adult lives working inside the home. At the very least, such women should not be pushed into straitened circumstances by divorce. But that is what's happening in all too many cases.

No-fault is part of the problem, but issues unrelated to the grounds for divorce also contribute to unfair outcomes. As many experts have observed, the law of divorce has failed long-married women twice over—by allowing men expanded opportunities for nonconsensual divorce and by not specifying appropriate terms of financial rectification. The exercise of judicial discretion within the no-fault framework has failed to protect the vulnerable. Settlements based on the principle of formal equality have not recognized the fact of structural inequality.

Two changes could help address this situation. First, the possibility of long-term alimony (which has all but vanished from contemporary settlements) should be restored for women who have invested heavily in the marriage at the expense of their opportunities outside the home.

...

Second, even when fault is not legally relevant as grounds for divorce, it may well be appropriate to take it into account in determining fair settlements.

...

The proposed changes in settlements involving children and women in long-established marriages would protect the economic interests of these two vulnerable groups. The changes would also put men on notice that the financial responsibilities they will bear after divorce are considerable and long-term. It is not unreasonable to expect, then, that the combination of new limits on no-fault and more stringent settlement principles will have a deterrent effect, reducing the incidence of divorce.

The Moral Challenge

The law, however, is a limited instrument of social policy. At some point, highly demanding laws become less effective than those that are less restrictive. The identification of the optimal level of legal restraint is a matter of art rather than of science. Experience suggests that the optimum will fall well short of our hopes.

In the end, the future of marriage in America hinges on a handful of moral questions. Are we willing to put the well-being of children first, even when this conflicts with adult desires and restrains our current passion for unfettered autonomy? Are we willing to honor claims of justice and fairness in the case of those who have sacrificed personal advancement for the good of the family? And are we prepared to recognize the kind of contentment that stems not from the gratification of momentary impulse but from loyalty to commitments that endure? Only when we are able, as a society, to return affirmative answers to these questions will reforms in the law of divorce have a real chance of success.

Love, American Style: What the Alarmists about Divorce Don't Get about Idealism in America

Margaret
Talbot

Every month for the past 44 years, the *Ladies' Home Journal* has soothed and titillated its readers with a column called "Can This Marriage Be Saved?," a feature that is today, as it has always been, a fervent tribute to the American faith in matrimony. By now, the question contained in the title is purely rhetorical: The troubled marriages brought to life through this pop opera for three voices—wife, husband, counselor—are always, always saved.

...

In the early 1950s, when the column first appeared, its wildly successful record of marriages reprieved might not have seemed so fanciful. Now, when half of all marriages in America end in divorce, "Can This Marriage Be Saved?" reads more like an exercise in nostalgia, or futile cultural stubbornness. In any event, the column's enduring popularity with its 5 million readers suggests the persistence of a set of beliefs: that marriages ought to be saved; that some of the worst of them can be saved; that, insofar as even these nuptial casualties can be rescued, so, surely, can the institution of marriage. The twin ideals here, shining like klieg lights through great cloud banks of misunderstanding, are the perfectibility and the desirability of marriage.

A pop cultural artifact such as "Can This Marriage Be Saved?" ought to present the divorce alarmists in our midst with a conundrum. If you accept the premise of the alarmists—that Americans are living now in a blighted postmarital landscape, where every signpost announces that marriage is disposable and divorce is a cinch—then how to explain this interminable valentine to the regenerative powers of marriage? How, for that matter, to explain the attitudes that most Americans still profess toward marriage, in poll after poll, at altar after altar? Despite the odds, and they are pretty formidable, 90 percent of men and women in the United States eventually marry. The percentage of Americans who say they want to marry has held steady, at 96 percent, for the last 30 years. Almost three-fourths of Americans, according to one recent survey, believe that "marriage is a life-long commitment that should not be ended except under extreme circumstances." Even the gay rights movement, once so dedicated to giddy non-monogamy, has lately got it bad for the honorable estate.

But there is a paradox. Marriage, you might say, is the underlying cause of divorce. The higher the expectations of marriage—one index, after all, of respect for the institution—the greater the number of divorces. Idealize marriage, and the real complications of love and sex and companionship and family will bite back.

...

It is not hard to see the ecumenical appeal of the antidivorce project. The right likes it because it is an issue best confronted by means of cultural retooling and individual initiative, not government programs. The communitarian left likes it because it allows them to train their ire on the "selfish" middle class, who contribute at least as much to rising divorce rates (unlike, say, rising illegitimacy rates) as the poor do. And both camps can easily fit it into a politically potent discourse about the decline of the family. Even many feminists like it, because the antidivorce movement extends an awkward gallantry to women, insisting that they are more likely than men to suffer the ill effects of marital breakups, and larding their writings with witticisms such as "a woman in favor of divorce is like a turkey in favor of Christmas." (Never mind that most divorces are initiated by women, and that in study after study more divorced women than divorced men say that they are glad to be out of their marriages.)

But the antidivorce movement owes most of its appeal—and most of its integrity—to the fact that on one point it is incontrovertibly correct: For children, divorce has serious, even dire, consequences. Divorce pushes many families into poverty, and it can be psychologically wounding, according to a growing pile of evidence, in ways that last well into adulthood. Children of divorce are less likely to graduate from high school, and they are more likely to get pregnant as teenagers than children whose married parents still live together. They are more prone to depression and even to joblessness. Their own marriages are more likely to fail.

...

With all of this to recommend the antidivorce movement, it has been easy to neglect the shortcomings of its arguments. The shortcomings are many. They begin with a reluctance to draw distinctions: between divorces that involve children and those that do not; between broken families whose parents never married in the first place and broken families whose parents are divorced; between divorces sought out of boredom and divorces sought out of soul-killing unhappiness. The divorcephobes also misread American history, in a manner that makes the sixties and its counterculture bulk absurdly large. And most enfeebling of all for their movement, they fail to summon up a vision of marriage more compelling than the one most Americans seem to share already, the one whose very strengths make it peculiarly vulnerable.

Since the mid-nineteenth century, the divorce rate in America has been climbing steadily. There have been peaks: in the 1880s, when Gilded Age marriages conceived in haste or in greed proved particularly combustible and 1 out of every 14 marriages ended in divorce, and in the immediate aftermath of both world wars. And there have been troughs: Fewer people divorced during the Depression, for instance, than before or since. The sharpest increase, though, began in the early 1960s, and roughly doubled the divorce rate, bringing it to an unprecedented high in 1981. The numbers have since leveled off, but they still translate into odds dooming half of all marriages.

. . .

Marriage here has always been less stable than it was in the Old World, because it has always been understood, in its model form anyway, to be a union of affectionate equals, rather than a melding of dynasties or a marmoreal hierarchy of male and female.... The love match, rather than the arranged marriage, has been the norm in the United States from its inception. And since love matches are inherently wobblier than arranged marriages, divorce has long been something of an American tradition, too.

It was the very uncountercultural Puritans who first introduced divorce to the American colonies. In cases of adultery or willful desertion, the courts and the legislatures of New England granted it from about 1620 onward. And, unlike their English equivalents, they allowed divorced spouses to marry again. (In England, the divorce "of bed-and-board," which permitted couples to live separately but not to remarry, was standard.) This willingness to countenance divorce, to treat it as a matter for civil courts rather than ecclesiastical courts, and to encourage new unions more securely bound by love, was accompanied by the hope that marriages would be the stronger and the sweeter for it. For love was incumbent upon the marriage contract, and a loveless marriage did no honor to God.

. . .

I don't mean to suggest that the Puritan view of marriage and divorce is our own view of marriage and divorce. We no longer take kindly to the culture of scarlet letters. (Not even to movies about them.) Still, there are elements of the Puritan dispensation—the tolerance for dissolving marriages in the interest of preserving marriage, the availability of divorce to rich and poor alike, the idea of tender friendship as the all-important bond uniting husband and wife—that render it more familiar to us than the Old World's contemporaneous view of these matters. In England, for example, the right to divorce, complete with permission for both parties to remarry, was not established until 1857, and even then it was mostly limited to the upper classes. In France and Germany, it came much later. And, as Edmund Morgan notes, "compared to a wife in contemporary England, the Puritan wife had a relatively enviable portion." Her husband could not lawfully strike her; she and he held positions of equal authority in relation to their children and servants; and, in case of divorce, she stood a better chance than her English counterpart of retaining some property.

···

Divorce was an expression of idealism about marriage, not a concession of realism about it. In a nation founded on the idea that it is better to dissolve an unfelicitous union than to swear a purely formal allegiance to it, divorce has long been defended with the ennobling rhetoric of freedom. Above all, though, this has meant the freedom to establish a more harmonious marriage, a marriage that would neither be corrupted by adultery nor corroded by lovelessness. "Liberty of divorce prevents and cures domestic quarrels," and thus "preserves liberty of affections," wrote Thomas Jefferson when, as a young lawyer, he prepared the divorce case of a client.

None of which is to say that divorce was widely accepted or common in the United States before our time, only that it was more widely accepted and more common than it was anywhere else. And it was becoming steadily more so. Divorced women might have been thought vulgar and divorced men caddish, but divorce itself was increasingly regarded as a necessary safety valve that preserved marriage even as it liberated individuals from lifetimes of misery. Consider, for example, the growing inventory of grievances for which divorce was the accepted remedy. Before the introduction of no-fault laws in the 1970s, the only way to get out of a marriage legally was to charge one's spouse with some egregious dereliction of duty.

···

In many ways, the no-fault laws that emerged in the seventies were a culmination of centuries of American thinking about marriage and divorce. "No-fault" was actually something of a misnomer. The idea wasn't so much to expunge the idea of fault as it was to suggest that fault in marriage, like fractures in a bone, was often compound. "No-fault" is shorthand for the recognition that in a failed marriage both parties are usually at fault, so that there is no point in prolonging the pain or the expense by denying the commonality of the failure.

···

Moreover, in removing the necessity for lawyers and courtrooms, no-fault laws were also meant to draw the venom from the most confrontational divorces. And the less venom, the better for any children involved.

···

Any argument about the evils of divorce rests, ultimately, on a vision of the good marriage. This is especially true for the current cohort of divorcephobes. They are not interested in compassionate reforms to soften the impact of divorce on children—stricter enforcement of child support payment, for example—so much as in drastically reducing divorce in the first place. Their goal is to make American marriages impervious to divorce. That is a little like trying to make stockings impervious to runs. It can probably be done, but only by coarsening the fabric.

…

It is hard to imagine this antidivorce vision of marriage doing a whole lot to boost the nuptial cause. Who wants to be a disabused bride or groom? (The antidivorce writers, you might say, are guilty of spousal disabuse.) With its joyless tsk-tskery about romantic love, its sanctimonious tributes to the sackcloth and ashes of a bad marriage, their vision is not exactly irresistible. The divorcephobes admire Japan, where divorces are indeed uncommon—but so, by most accounts, are openly affectionate marriages, or even marriages in which husband and wife spend much time together. They admire people who perversely settle down into what sound like mockeries of marriage, yoking themselves to spouses whom they have ceased to love or respect.

…

The critics of divorce are forever telling what are clearly meant to be morally heartening stories about husbands and wives (usually wives) who decide to stick it out with the jerks they married. But they don't seem to realize how hollow their exempla ring. There's Marie, for example, who, as Gallagher tells it, wants to leave her husband Mark. And who can blame her? In his late twenties, Mark went back to grad school, where he "drank heavily on occasion, dabbled in cocaine, and propositioned more than one young coed." Later, though Mark has trouble finding or keeping a job, and though Marie "endure[s] many more failures of love at his hands," they stay together because, as Mark puts it, "it was the white, upper-middle-class, Christian Republican thing to do." Eventually they are rewarded by finding some facsimile of love again. Gallagher declares the spectacle a "moving tribute to … strength of character." Well, maybe. I don't know Mark and Marie. It might have been more of a tribute to his or her strength of character if Mark had shaped up or Marie had shipped out. To what extent ought their kind of story be turned into a fable for the rest of us?

The same goes for the creepy little tale that opens a recent issue of *The American Enterprise* magazine devoted to divorce. Karl Zinsmeister, the editor, introduces us to Kevin, an acquaintance who sells cars. When Kevin starts an affair with a secretary at the dealership, his employer intervenes. And rather aggressively, as the admiring Zinsmeister explains.

They [his employers] know Kevin's wife, who is willing to take him back. They offered to give Kevin time off from work so the two of them could work their problems through. They offered to pay for them to take a trip together. They offered him money for counseling. They told Kevin that saving his marriage was worth it, and important to them as his employer. And when Kevin refused their offers of help, they fired him and the secretary he was consorting with. They contested his application for unemployment benefits on the grounds that he hadn't been laid off but rather dismissed for refusing to follow company standards of personal conduct. In our small town, I'd say there's a pretty good chance they let other potential employers know what they thought about the man.

Poor Kevin. I had to read the article several times before I realized that Zinsmeister was presenting this disturbing tale—Shirley Jackson by way of Lee Kwan Yew—in a positive light. He was happy to see a private company assume the role of morally vetting and socioeconomically punishing the personal conduct of its employees.

The antidivorce movement is big on this sort of thing. Marriage, we are instructed, is about more than two people, and so the "community" must tromp in to shore it up. And that might work, if the community that communitarianism fetishized actually existed—if, for example, couples lived in the bosom of snoopy extended families and concerned neighbors, all with elaborate financial, social, and religious investments in keeping them married. But outside of a few immigrant cultures, most Americans never lived in large extended families. (Outside of a few totalitarian societies, few people have lived at all placidly amid such intrusive neighbors.) And the general and seemingly irreversible trend in American social life has been toward greater social isolation (and individual freedom and privacy)—a trend that reached its apogee in the suburban migration of the fifties, the very decade for which antidivorce types are so nostalgic.

...

It's odd: For all their talk about strengthening marriage, the antidivorcers have almost nothing to say about the love between husband and wife. In fact, they frequently write in the icy, off-putting tone of the social engineer. For them, marriage is primarily a social institution, designed for the efficient rearing of children, and for the transmission of values. Marriage is these things, of course; but it is also, and fundamentally, a sacrament between two people. Surely something is lost in a vision of marriage that is so willing to make do with the mere appearance of love between its protagonists, that seems to set so much store by the preservation of norms and forms and so little store by the heart. Not the therapeutic heart. The human heart.

A couple that marries so one of them can get a green card, or (as Peruvian law allows) so that a rapist can expunge his crime by wedding his victim—it's hard to find anything in the polemics against divorce that would definitively exclude such matches from the respect that they accord all legal marriage. If love is not the crucial element, after all, then many other things can be.

These writers who make a career out of paradise lost could do worse than have another look at John Milton. "Marriage," he wrote,

> is a covenant the very being whereof consists not in a forced cohabitation and counterfeit performance of duties, but in unfeigned love and peace ... love in marriage cannot live nor subsist unless it be mutual; and where love cannot be, there can be left of wedlock nothing but the empty husk of an outside matrimony, as undelightful and unpleasing to God as any other kind of hypocrisy.

Key Websites

CAN THE GOVERNMENT PREVENT DIVORCE?

Francine Russo, *Can the Government Prevent Divorce?*: Researchers say that states can—and some states feel they should—reduce the likelihood of divorce by altering the course of bad marriages in the making. Russo believes that with the costs of divorce now estimated to be in the billions annually, a modest investment in divorce reduction would make sense.
http://www.theatlantic.com/issues/97oct/divorce.htm

COVENANT MARRIAGE LINKS

Developed by the Americans for Divorce Reform group, this site, devoted to covenant marriage, is intended to bring together a great deal of information about this practice that makes divorce more difficult to obtain. The site includes links to legislation, news, opinions, and scholarly articles. It also explores the history of the idea of covenant marriage.
http://www.divorcereform.org/cov.html

THE LIMITS OF THE LIMITS ON DIVORCE

Robert M. Gordon, *The Limits of the Limits on Divorce*: Gordon argues that highly restrictive divorce laws would have little effect on divorce rates but would impose large costs on children. Contrary to the claims by some of no-fault's critics, recent research shows that while some children suffer serious harm from divorce, other children benefit from divorce. Compared to cultural and economic influences, the law has a small influence on rates of marital breakdown.
http://www.divorcenet.com/famlaw/famlaw09.html

NATIONAL VITAL STATISTICS REPORTS, VOLUME 47, NUMBER 1 TO PRESENT

This site provides data on births, marriages, divorces, and teenage pregnancy in the United States.
http://www.cdc.gov/nchs/products/pubs/pubd/nvsr/47-pre/47-pre.htm

CORNELL UNIVERSITY LAW SCHOOL LEGAL INFORMATION INSTITUTE

This site contains commentary and primary source material about divorce law. The pages provide information on federal and state law, statutes, regulations, and other related sources.
http://www.law.cornell.edu/topics/divorce.html

U.S. SUPREME COURT: RECENT DIVORCE DECISIONS

This site provides a review of Supreme Court decisions that have an impact on divorce in the United States.
http://www4.law.cornell.edu/cgi-bin/fx?DB=SupctSyllabi&TOP-DOC=0&P=divorce

DIVORCE CENTRAL

This site features information in four topic-specific areas: the legal center, the lifeline (for emotional support), the parenting center, and the financial center. Each center includes information, bulletin boards for posting questions or comments, numerous articles, checklists, and links to other sites.
http://www.divorcecentral.com

Should Limits Be Placed on the Use of Reproductive Technology?

Colonial Americans took seriously the biblical mandate to increase and multiply. And with good reason—many children died at birth or in infancy, and new hands were always needed to work the farm and keep the house.

From their pulpits, Puritan preachers such as Cotton Mather cautioned their flocks that being "barren" meant that God had cast a dark judgment upon them. Other clergymen took a less punitive view, believing that childlessness was a sign that the couple's lives had another purpose.

Childlessness brought suspicion on someone in the colonial period. If a couple was childless, generally the woman was held responsible, as infertility was thought to be a woman's problem.

Even the first president of the United States openly expressed such a prejudice. George and Martha Washington never had any children of their own. Before marrying Martha, George Washington battled smallpox and fevers that may have left him infertile. But in a letter to his nephew, the president made it clear he thought Martha the barren one—even though she had conceived four times before marrying him. The children playing at George Washington's Virginia plantation, Mount Vernon, were actually Martha's children by a previous marriage. General Washington treated those children as his own.

Our society continues to define parenthood in terms of procreation. The infertile look for ever-more-elaborate forms of high-tech treatment. When people who have been trying to have a baby realize there is something wrong, they usually consult the family doctor and then a fertility specialist. They then learn about the various options open to them and proceed along the high-tech fertility road. We have developed a complicated child production market in which eggs, embryos, sperm, and pregnancy services are for sale so that those who want to become parents have a variety of options. The assisted reproductive technology business is a $2 billion a year industry that produces nearly 100,000 births.

At the same time, we do little to encourage parents to adopt the children who already exist. Adoption agencies do not encourage adoption until the couple is sure that they have resolved their fertility issues. In effect, society gives a very clear message that adoption is an inferior form of parenting and should be thought of as a last resort.

Part of the reason we give preferential treatment to those seeking to become biological parents is that they operate in a free-market world in which they are able to make their own decisions, subject only to financial and physical restraints. Those seeking to adopt operate in a highly regulated world in which government intervenes to determine who will be allowed to become a parent. The parental screening requirement of many agencies deters many who might otherwise consider adoption. By subjecting adoptive but not biological parents to screening, society suggests that it trusts people who raise a birth child, but distrusts what goes on when a child is transferred from a birth parent to an adoptive parent.

In this chapter, the authors discuss the question of whether limits should be placed on the use of reproductive technology. Law professor Lori B. Andrews, in her book *The Clone Age: Adventures in the New Age of Reproductive Technology*, contends that new reproductive and genetic technologies are being offered without sufficient thought about their impact or desirability. Not only are there many ethical issues to consider, but unlike new drugs and medical equipment, which are regulated by the Food and Drug Administration, innovative reproductive technology procedures are not subject to review. Andrews thinks it is time for us to reconsider our headlong pursuit of new procedures in this area.

Karen Wright and Sarah Richardson, in their article "Human in the Age of Mechanical Reproduction," disagree. They believe couples should be able to pursue the birth of a child with whatever methods become available. They recognize that the rapid advances in assisted reproductive technology techniques produce complicated ethical and legal issues. Resolving them, however, should fall to future generations, since it will be the children of assisted reproduction who will have to pass judgment on the technology that helped create them.

Yes

Lori B.
Andrews

The Clone Age: Adventures in the New Age of Reproductive Technology

Everywhere I look, new reproductive and genetic technologies are being offered, without sufficient thought about their impact or desirability.

...

My phone rings daily with calls from journalists, judges, and government agencies wanting my opinion on the latest technology. GIFT, ZIFT, ICSI, the number of acronyms grows. The Japanese have tried this, the South Koreans that. I feel as if the world is locked into a battle over who can push the boundaries the farthest.

...

In the course of my career, I have learned several truisms: If it has worked in just one animal, it will be tried in a woman. If a baby is born from the technique, her picture will go up on the clinic wall, but no one will study how she fares as she develops, nor how her mother does over time.

...

And what about the women? They are trapped in an endless cycle of trying. Just when they think they are ready to come to terms with their infertility and remain childless or adopt, their doctors offer a new acronym. Those baby photos on the clinic wall stare down at them. "Quitter ... failure," they seem to chant. So the women give it another go.

When I first entered the field, in vitro fertilization was used only on women with hopelessly damaged fallopian tubes who needed it to circumvent their infertility. The doctors told me it would be *unethical* to subject a fertile women to the risk of hormonal stimulation, retrieval of eggs, and so forth, to address her husband's infertility. Instead, the couple could create a child through artificial insemination by donor, a widely accepted, safe procedure at a cost less than a tenth as much as IVF, with a much higher success rate and less risk to women.

But that moral boundary did not last for long. In 1993, doctors began offering ICSI—intracytoplasmic sperm injection—to couples where the husband had a low sperm count. Even though the wife didn't need it, she was put through all the rigors of IVF so that her eggs could be harvested and directly injected in vitro with her husband's sperm. Where, previously, a man was considered infertile unless he produced millions of sperm per ejaculate, now a man can be fertile even if he can produce only a single sperm.

For the doctors in the lab, the procedure itself was thrilling. They took a thin needle and shot the sperm into the egg. It was like sex under the microscope.

There was in fact something so satisfying about controlling conception that the doctors started using ICSI even in cases where the husband produced enough sperm to fertilize an in vitro egg without the injection. Within four years, more than one-third of all IVF procedures involved ICSI. Tens of thousands of children were born after ICSI.

In Belgium and Australia—unlike the United States—the government keeps track of how many children conceived through reproductive techniques have genetic abnormalities. In 1998, researchers in those countries noticed that the children created by ICSI were twice as likely to have major chromosomal abnormalities as were children conceived naturally. At age one, the children of ICSI showed developmental delays in problem-solving ability, memory, and language skills compared to children conceived through sex or IVF.

When ICSI is used because the father has inheritable infertility, his sons will be infertile and will need to use ICSI to reproduce as well. So, with each procedure, the clinic is creating a new generation of clients.

ICSI is not the only technique being used without sufficient advance study. The lack of regulation of fertility and genetic techniques means doctors can introduce experimental procedures into their clinical practice soon after they are invented, often long before they have been adequately researched in animals.

...

For men who don't produce sperm, Ralph Brinster of the University of Pennsylvania Veterinary School suggests taking immature cells from the man's testes and maturing them in a pig's or bull's testes, which would then produce human sperm. Other researchers suggest a more promising alternative to the artificial womb: gestating human fetuses in animals of a compatible species, such as cows.

"Part of the way we think about who we are and how we value ourselves has to do with our origins and reproduction," says bioethicist Arthur

Caplan. "Something is challenging the specialness of humanity if you originate human beings in some animal's reproductive tract."

When the problem is with the woman's egg rather than the husband's
sperm, an egg donor can be used. But donated eggs from women volunteers
are scarce, with prices escalating up to $5,000 per egg. So a search has begun
for alternative sources of genetic material to produce babies.

Researchers are focusing on the biological fact that all of a woman's
eggs are created prenatally. A woman actually has her maximum number of
eggs—about 7 million—when she is a 20-week-old fetus in her mother's
womb. By puberty, only around 300,000 remain, and up to 400 will be ovu-
lated before she reaches menopause.

With a million abortions a year, some scientists have begun to think the
unthinkable—using female fetuses as a source of eggs for infertile women.

Immature eggs can be harvested from an aborted fetus and matured in
a laboratory. The eggs can then be used in a regular in vitro fertilization
process. Another variation is to transplant pieces of a fetal ovary into a woman
whose ovaries are not working or are not present.

...

Concerns were raised about the psychological impact on the child, who
some said would grow up knowing that "his grandmother murdered his
mother." How would the child feel? While learning that her genetic mother
was a dead fetus might not be the same type of loss as the death of a mother she knew and loved, a child might nonetheless grieve. She might feel angry
at her biological grandmother for consenting to the abortion or receiving
money for the eggs, which prevented her mother from living.

Others counter that, while the idea is troubling at first glance, the reasonable child will come to realize that life is better than no life.

...

And then there is the next logical extension: A woman who cannot
produce eggs could be cloned, carry the cloned fetus for a few months, then
abort it to remove its ovaries. Her IVF doctor would harvest eggs, which would
be identical to those the woman's ovaries would have produced. The doctor
would then fertilize the eggs from the abortus with her husband's sperm in
vitro to create the children she and her husband would otherwise have had.

Yet there is a complex concern about what this line of research says
about females. The process, says lawyer Adrienne Davis, transforms fetuses
from a mass of cells to "gendered being." They become girls who would have
grown up to become women and who would have been able to make their
own reproductive decisions such as whether to procreate or not. The har-
vesting of eggs might move us closer to "fetal farming," possibly turning fetuses into a source for spare body parts.

...

Also pushing social boundaries is the possibility of male pregnancy. A
man could be primed with an injection of female hormones, and then an in

vitro embryo could be inserted into his abdominal cavity. A placenta would develop and, with luck, attach to the omentum, a fatty, blood-rich tissue that hangs in front of the intestines. Nine months later, the baby could be extracted in a procedure akin to a cesarean section.

...

The logic of male pregnancy seems quite similar to that of having the wife of an infertile male undergo in vitro fertilization because of her husband's infertility. In such a case, the woman undergoes hormonal stimulation and other procedures to avoid using a third party, the sperm donor. With male pregnancy, if the woman has an infertility problem preventing gestation, her husband can carry the fetus to avoid the use of a surrogate mother.

"If we are truly a society based on constitutional equality, regardless of race, religion or sex, then that is exactly what should happen," one doctor wrote to me, emphasizing that the right to use reproductive technologies should belong to men as well as women.

...

The fact that most researchers and doctors are male obviously influences the technologies that are available. Men don't even have to take fertility drugs: It's the women (and the children) who are at risk with most reproductive technologies.

...

Unlike new drugs and new medical equipment, which are regulated by the Food and Drug Administration, no similar review of innovative reproductive technology procedures is required. Reproductive technologies also differ from other medical procedures because they are rarely covered by health insurance; only a dozen states' laws mandate infertility coverage. For other types of health services, health insurers, through managed care outcome studies and evaluation of services, have required certain proof of efficacy before medical services are reimbursed.

Additionally, medical malpractice litigation, which serves as a quality control mechanism in other areas of health care, does not work as well in this field. The normal success rates for the procedures (25 percent for in vitro, for example) are so low that it makes it difficult to prove the doctor was negligent. Risks to the children may not be discernible for many years, which may be past the period of time a statute of limitations on a legal suit has run. In "wrongful life" cases, courts have been reluctant to impose liability upon medical providers and labs for children born with birth defects where the child would not have been born if the negligent act had been avoided; only three states recognize such a cause of action. Consequently, experimental techniques are rapidly introduced in the more than 300 high-tech infertility clinics in the United States without sufficient prior animal experimentation, randomized clinical trials, or the rigorous data collection that would occur in other types of medical experimentation. This is truly the Wild West of medicine.

Should it be up to individual doctors to decide which new technologies should be used to create the next generation? In other areas of medicine, that is not the case. Most medical research in university and other hospitals is initially funded by the federal government through the National Institutes of Health and, by law, must be reviewed in advance by a neutral committee, an Institutional Review Board, before it can be tried in humans. Since reproductive technologies have been held hostage to the abortion debate, they have not received federal funds. Researchers can still submit their plans to hospital and university Institutional Review Boards, but they usually do not.

...

Reproductive technology is tougher to regulate than nuclear technology. The tools for reproductive technology are relatively inexpensive and widely available. "A reprogenetics clinic could easily be run on the scale of a small business anywhere in the world," notes Princeton biologist Lee Silver. There are IVF clinics in at least 38 countries, from Malaysia to Pakistan and Thailand to Egypt.

In the United States, the assisted reproductive technology industry, with an annual revenue of $2 billion, is growing to serve the estimated one in six American couples of reproductive age who are infertile. Annually, in the United States alone, approximately 60,000 births result from donor insemination, 15,000 from IVF, and at least 1,000 from surrogacy arrangements. In contrast, only about 30,000 healthy infants are available for adoption. What is so striking about this comparison is that every state has an elaborate regulatory mechanism in place for adoption while only three states, Florida, Virginia, and New Hampshire, have enacted legislation to comprehensively address assisted reproductive technologies. And they aren't even the states where the most high-tech reproduction is conducted!

...

"The great challenge to mankind today is not only how to create, but to know when to stop creating," said Lord Emmanuel Jacobovitz, former chief rabbi of Britain, when he heard about the possibility of using fetal eggs. "And, when we celebrate a Sabbath to remind ourselves that God initially created this world, we celebrate not his act of creation on the six days. We celebrate that he knew when to stop."

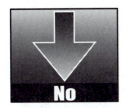

Human in the Age
of Mechanical Reproduction

**Karen Wright
and Sarah
Richardson**

"Mommy, where do babies come from?"

Parents have dreaded this question ever since the stork made its first delivery. But today's mommies and daddies have more explaining to do than their own parents could possibly have imagined. Though the birds and bees discussion was never easy, its elements were fairly straightforward: the fireworks exploding, the train chugging through the tunnel, the waves pounding the shore, the occasional reference to anatomy. Once upon a time, baby-making was synonymous with whoopee-making, and frozen eggs were for pastry dough, and seven was how many times you should let the phone ring before you hang up, not how many fetuses you could fit in a womb.

These days, though, the facts of life can sound a lot like science fiction, as late-twentieth-century humanity grapples with the rise of noncoital conception. There are now more than a dozen ways to make a baby, the vast majority of which bypass the antiquated act of sexual congress. The last three decades have seen the advent of such high-tech interventions as fertility drugs, in vitro fertilization, donor eggs, donor sperm, donor embryos, and surrogate mothering. In the works are still more advanced technologies, such as the transfer of cell nuclei, embryo splitting, and even, if at least one man has his way, the cloning of human adults.

These techniques generally are gathered under the heading of "assisted reproduction." All the ones in use today were pioneered for and are usually employed by infertile couples of childbearing age. But they are also used by people with less conventional notions of parenting—singles, post-menopausal women, and gay partners. In the near future, assisted reproduction may become standard procedure for anyone who wants to conceive and who can afford it. The allure, of course, is control: control over the timing of parenthood, control over "embryo quality," control over genetic disease, control over less pernicious characteristics, such as gender, that are also determined by genes.

So far, owing to federal policy and societal preference, the practice of assisted reproduction is largely unregulated. One specialist has even called it the Wild West of medicine. It's also expensive, bothersome, inefficient, and fraught with ethical complications—but none of those considerations has slowed its growth. Since 1978, when the first test-tube baby was born, the number of fertility clinics in the United States has gone from less than 30 to more than 300. The multibillion-dollar fertility industry has created tens of thousands of babies. Assisted reproduction has relieved the anguish of men and women who, just decades ago, would have had to abandon their hopes of having children. It's also created a world where a dead man can impregnate a stranger, where a woman can rent out her uterus, and where a child can have five parents—and still end up an orphan. It's not at all clear how this new world will change the meaning of family. But it has already transformed what used to be known as the miracle of birth.

...

IVF [in vitro fertilization] is the cornerstone of assisted reproductive technology. The procedure—in which ripe eggs are removed from the ovaries and incubated with sperm—greatly improves the haphazard gambit of traditional in vivo fertilization. It also introduces another level of complexity and expense. In addition to egg-ripening hormones, a woman undergoing IVF will usually take a protean cocktail of drugs designed to suppress and then trigger the release of mature eggs. Egg retrieval, done by guiding a hollow needle through the wall of the vagina and into the nearby ovaries, is characterized as a minor surgical procedure.

...

GIFT [gamete intrafallopian transfer] is one of several variations on the IVF theme that were introduced in the 1980s as infertility specialists sought to expand their skills in assisted reproduction.... Even with these innovations, however, the efficacy of assisted reproduction is sobering.... Success rates for IVF depend on a patient's age and vary from clinic to clinic and from procedure to procedure. But the ballpark figure—the so-called take-home baby rate—is one live birth for every five IVF cycles. Infertility specialists point out that the success rates for these procedures increase every year and that in any given month a fertile couple's chance of conceiving by traditional means is also one in five. According to the American Society for Reproductive Medicine, more than half of all infertile couples could attain pregnancy if they persisted long enough with treatments for assisted reproduction.

But that also means that about half will never have a baby, no matter how much therapy they get. And one thing about making babies by the usual means is that it's free. If at first you don't succeed, you can try, try again, without taking out a second mortgage. A single cycle of IVF, on the other hand, costs between $8,000 and $10,000. Special options like GIFT may cost more.

...

Is it worth it? The market says yes. Although rates of infertility have remained constant, demand for infertility services has risen steadily in the past two decades. Today about 6 million couples in the United States have fertility problems; half of them go to their doctors for help, and about a quarter end up trying assisted reproduction.

...

Moreover, pursuing parenthood via assisted reproduction means being confronted with ethical decisions well outside the range of most people' s moral radars. Because IVF techniques often give rise to multiple pregnancies, selective reduction is an issue here as well. Couples undergoing IVF must also decide how many eggs to fertilize and transfer at one time (which bears on the question of multiple pregnancy), whether they want to create and freeze embryos for future use, and what the eventual disposition of any unused frozen embryos should be. Former spouses have waged custody battles over frozen embryos, and in at least one case the attending IVF clinic claimed the embryo as its lawful property. Legally, human embryos occupy a gray area all their own, somewhere between human life and some rarefied form of property.

Assisted reproduction also invites the preselection of embryos based on genetic traits, and all the moral dilemmas that may accrue thereto. Screening is done by removing a single cell from an eight-cell embryo and analyzing the chromosomes or DNA in the cell nucleus. Already some clinics offer to screen in vitro embryos for genes related to cystic fibrosis, hemophilia, and muscular dystrophy. Couples can decide which of the embryos they've created meet their specifications; the rejected embryos can be discarded or donated to research.

Finally, assisted reproduction has opened the door to all manner of gamete swapping and surrogacy, from the simplest and oldest method—artificial insemination with a donor's sperm—to more complex scenarios in which any combination of donor eggs, donor sperm, and donor embryos may be used. In addition to biological surrogate motherhood (the method that created the celebrated Baby M), "gestational surrogates" will agree to carry and give birth to a baby to whom they bear no genetic relation whatsoever. It is now possible for a person to "have" a baby by procuring eggs and sperm from donors and hiring a "birth mother" to do the rest (this has been done). It is possible for a woman to use a birth mother for cosmetic reasons or convenience alone (this has also been done). It is possible for the sperm of dead men to be retrieved and used to impregnate their widows (likewise). It is possible for women long past the age of menopause to give birth (this, too, has already happened).

...

Once it becomes widely available, cryopreservation will offer a unique opportunity to women: the chance to store their young eggs for use at a later date. Defects in aging eggs are thought to be responsible for the declining fertility of older women; indeed, donor-egg technology has demonstrated that the rest of the female reproductive apparatus withstands the test of time. By assuring women a lifetime of viable gametes, egg freezing could let them beat the biological clock.

Of course, women would then be using assisted reproduction for their own convenience rather than for treatment of an existing medical condition. In this respect, egg freezing echoes a common theme in assisted reproduction. Current techniques were developed to help patients with specific medical problems—egg freezing, for example, will allow cancer patients whose eggs would be destroyed by radiation to set aside some gametes prior to therapy. Yet inevitably, the fruits of infertility research expand reproductive options for all men and women. And these choices are not always easy to live with, for individuals or for society.

...

Critics of assisted reproduction fear that today's innovations will become tomorrow's imperatives. Already some infertile couples feel entrapped by the catalog of choices. "All these technologies, by providing more and more options, make it very difficult to say, 'No, we've tried enough,'" says R. Alta Charo, a law professor at the University of Wisconsin and member of the National Bioethics Advisory Commission. "Choice is not a bad thing—but neither is it an unalloyed good."

...

And lack of regulation only exacerbates the problems surrounding assisted reproduction. "This field is screaming for regulation, oversight, and control," says Arthur Caplan, a noted bioethicist at the University of Pennsylvania. "What keeps us from doing so is the notion that individuals should have procreative freedom."

Rancor over abortion has also impeded the regulation of technologies for assisted reproduction. Since the 1970s, the United States has outlawed federal funding of research on human embryos or fetal tissue in response to concerns that such research would encourage trafficking in embryos and fetuses. The ban has not been applied to privately funded efforts, however; consequently, most research on assisted reproduction has been conducted beyond the reach of federal regulation and oversight.

Specialists in assisted reproduction ... say this is just as well—that regulators wouldn't appreciate the technical and moral complexities of the work.

But with the bulk of experimentation going on in private clinics, patients—and their children—can become guinea pigs. Even when couples are not directly involved in experimental procedures, they may be confronted with uncomfortable choices, such as financial incentives to donate their gametes or embryos.

...

Many observers fear that it is not the participants in assisted reproduction but their children who may suffer most from the imprudent use of these new technologies. For example, with the rising popularity of assisted reproduction, more and more children are being exposed to the risks of premature birth: Since 1971 the annual number of multiple births in the United States has more than quadrupled. Scientists and ethicists alike have spoken out against helping single, postmenopausal mothers conceive, arguing that it is morally reprehensible to create children who may well be orphaned. Some question the wisdom of arrangements—like surrogacy or gamete donation—that could diffuse the responsibility of parenthood. And some researchers are concerned with the safety of the procedures themselves for assisted reproduction. A recent—and controversial—Australian study of 420 children suggests that babies produced with the aid of intracytoplasmic sperm injection, in which a single sperm is injected into an incubating egg cell, are twice as likely to suffer major birth defects of the heart, genitals, and digestive tract.

...

Other commentators note that the rights of participants and progeny in assisted reproduction are still undefined. Laws vary widely from state to state on whether a child conceived by donor insemination has the right to know the identity of her biological father. "We never resolved the issues surrounding artificial insemination," says George Annas, a professor of law, medicine, and public health at Boston University. "We just act like we did. And then we import these issues into the new technology."

With the rapid advances in assisted-reproduction techniques, the ethical and legal issues can only become more complicated, and the task of resolving them will fall to future generations. But that may be fitting, if it's the children of assisted reproduction who pass judgment on the technology that helped create them.

KEY WEBSITES

TASC: THE AMERICAN SURROGACY CENTER, INC.

This website disseminates information on the third-party reproductive options of surrogacy and egg donation via the Internet and World Wide Web. Its mission is to offer information, professional resources, and the opportunity to connect with others who are pursuing these options. It includes several online support and e-mail discussion groups as well as Virtual Seminars hosted by professionals in various fields related to the topic of interest.
http://www.surrogacy.com

THE INTERNATIONAL COUNCIL FOR INFERTILITY INFORMATION DISSEMINATION (INCIID)

The InterNational Council for Infertility Information Dissemination (INCIID—pronounced "inside") is a nonprofit organization committed to providing the most current information regarding the diagnosis, treatment, and prevention of infertility and pregnancy loss. INCIID's purpose is entirely educational.
http://www.inciid.org

SOME OBSERVATIONS CONCERNING THE LAW OF SURROGACY

Mark A. Johnson, *Some Observations Concerning the Law of Surrogacy*: There is no unified body of law concerning surrogacy. It is an area in a constant state of flux, where traditional family-building approaches are being buffeted by newly available technological procedures and by the decisions of infertile couples to act upon them. This paper presents an overview of the history and issues involved.
http://www.surrogacy.com/legals/article/checklist/chklst1.html#IN FO_SOURCE

FERTILITY AND REPRODUCTIVE HEALTH NEWS

This site presents news about advances in reproductive health, studies, discoveries, and announcements.
http://www.inciid.org/fertinews/index.html

CENTERS FOR DISEASE CONTROL AND PREVENTION: ASSISTED REPRODUCTIVE TECHNOLOGY SUCCESS RATES

A woman's chances of having a pregnancy and a live birth using assisted reproductive technology are related to a variety of factors outside a clinic's control. Some of the factors covered in this report include the woman's age, the

cause of infertility, and the number of children that the woman has already had. The national data are useful because they can give potential reproductive technology users an idea of their chances of success. The data for this national report come from the 300 fertility clinics in operation in 1996 that provided and verified data on the outcomes of all ART cycles started in their clinics in 1996. Most of these clinics are members of the Society for Assisted Reproductive Technology (SART).
http://www.cdc.gov/nccdphp/drh/art96/index.htm

ETHICAL ASPECTS OF REPRODUCTIVE TECHNOLOGY

Our world has experienced a reproductive revolution starting with the birth control pill and in vitro fertilization and recently achieving a new level of success with the cloning of the first adult mammal, Dolly the sheep. To understand how and when to use reproductive technology, a critical ethical evaluation of the technology is necessary. The study of ethics involves examining traditions of belief about right and wrong human conduct, the interplay of social conduct and the impact of actions on others, and individual rights versus social cooperation in the context of moral, legal, and social principles.
http://www.molbio.princeton.edu/mb427/1997/students/
reproethics/main.html

Have We Exaggerated the Extent of Domestic Violence?

We hear a great deal today about domestic abuse and violence. Historically, wife beating was not considered to be a serious problem, and husband abuse was not even conceived of at all. Judges, particularly in the early 1800s, tended to think of domestic violence as a personal matter. It was thought that the courts should stay out of the conflict as long as the beating was "moderate" and only a matter of discipline—something akin to correcting a child. A writer in 1856 noted that a "brute in human form" who undertook to "chastise a vicious horse" would end up in prison, but not "one out of a hundred" of the men who abused or beat their wives (unless the wives were maimed or blinded) was brought to trial; and if he was, "he is sure of getting off by the payment of a small fine."

Later in the century a shift in attitudes took place, and a number of states passed statutes that made wife beating a crime. Nevada passed a law in 1877 that ordered every county to erect "in some public locality" a "substantial wooden post or stone pillar." Any "male person" above 18 "who shall willfully and violently strike, beat, or torture the body of any maiden or woman" 16 or older was to be "lashed in a standing posture to the post or pillar" for at least two hours, wearing on his chest a placard with the words *woman beater* or *wife beater* as the case might be. There is no evidence that this law was actually enforced. Other states went further and called for actual flogging of men who beat their wives.

Laws forbidding violence against women expressed an ideal, but, in practice, it is not clear whether these laws accomplished very much. Although some men did go to jail, wives were often reluctant or too terrified to complain or testify against their husbands. Sometimes outsiders stepped in and provided assistance.

It was also thought that wife beating was a brutal aberration. The popular image of the wife beater was that of an undisciplined beast with stubble on his chin. "Nice" men did not beat their wives.

It was not until the twentieth century, when feminists put forward the view that male dominance was the problem, that the issue was taken somewhat seriously. Domestic violence is, by and large, a secret vice, which makes it hard to chart its ebbs and flows.

Cathy Young, in her essay "Domestic Violations," contends that in order to punish spousal abuse, laws have been created that run roughshod over common sense and the rights of both men and women. She notes that the campaign against domestic violence has been heavily influenced by political motives that tend to frame the issue as a war of men against women. The laws ignore the fact that a great deal of domestic violence is reciprocal and that women commit as much of it as men. Young believes that men have been the victims of the war on domestic violence.

Diana Zuckerman and Stacey Friedman, in their paper "Measuring the Cost of Domestic Violence against Women," point out that domestic violence is extensive and costs society enormous amounts of money. They cite various studies to show that about 10 percent of all women experience husband-to-wife violence and approximately 20 percent of the adult female population are physically abused by a male intimate in their lifetime.

The costs of domestic violence include such direct costs as health care, foster care for children, homelessness, and incarceration. The indirect costs include job loss, lost productivity, and disruptions at the workplace when abusers harass the victim at work.

Yes

Cathy
Young

Domestic Violations

To punish spouse abuse, the law runs roughshod over common sense and the rights of both women and men.

In the fall of 1996, Susan Finkelstein's live-in boyfriend was arrested and charged with abusing her.

...

It all started when Susan and her boyfriend, a 44-year-old college administrator whom I'll call Jim, were having a heated argument on the way home from a party. Both of them, Susan explains, were under a great deal of stress. The quarrel escalated, and Jim decided it would be best to pull over. He wanted to get out of the car and walk, and Susan tried to stop him. "I lost my temper, he lost his temper, and we got into a mutual scuffle," she says. "I may have scratched him, he may have pushed me. It got physical, but there certainly wasn't any beating."

Finally, they cooled down and got back on the road—only to be stopped by a police car. Susan remembers thinking that Jim might have been driving erratically during the fight and might have looked like a drunk driver. But it was something very different. A passing motorist had seen their altercation, written down their license plate number, and called the police.

Despite Susan's assurances that Jim hadn't hurt her and she wasn't afraid of him, he was handcuffed and taken away. Under department policy, an officer told her, they had to make an arrest in a domestic dispute. Says

From *Reason*, 29 (February 1, 1998). Copyright © 1998 by Reason Foundation. Reprinted with the permission of Reason Foundation, 3415 South Sepulveda Blvd., Suite 400, Los Angeles, CA 90034. www.reason.com

Susan, "I was very upset that they wouldn't listen when I said that I was fine. They said, 'Well, we know that women who are abused often lie out of fear.'"

After spending the night in jail, Jim was arraigned on a misdemeanor charge of domestic violence and prohibited from having any contact with Susan, who had to stay with a friend. Her efforts to convince the judge and the prosecutor that nothing had happened were fruitless.

On a lawyer's advice, Jim pleaded no contest. He had to write a letter of apology to Susan (which he wrote in her presence and mailed to the district attorney's office, which forwarded it to her) and attend 10 weekly counseling sessions for batterers, a three-hour drive away, at a cost of $400. He is acutely aware that his record puts him at risk: "If Susan and I have a loud argument and a neighbor calls the police, I'll be arrested immediately," he says.

What happened to Jim and Susan—who are still together as a couple—is not an aberration. It's just another story from the trenches of what might be called the War on Domestic Violence. Born partly in response to an earlier tendency to treat wife beating as nothing more than a marital sport, this campaign treats all relationship conflict as a crime. The zero-tolerance mentality of current domestic violence policy means that no offense is too trivial, not only for arrest but for prosecution.

···

Like many crusades to stamp out social evils, the War on Domestic Violence is a mix of good intentions (who could be against stopping spousal abuse?), bad information, and worse theories. The result has been a host of unintended consequences that do little to empower victims while sanctioning state interference in personal relationships.

The battered women's advocacy movement, which has led the campaign against domestic abuse, is heavily influenced by radical feminist politics and tends to frame the issue in terms of a male "war against women." The mission statement of the National Coalition Against Domestic Violence links "violence against women and children" to "sexism, racism, classism, anti-Semitism, able-bodyism, ageism and other oppressions." Booklets funded by government and by charities such as United Way assert that "battering is the extreme expression of the belief in male dominance over women."

Such thinking is responsible for such widely circulated factoids as "domestic violence is the leading cause of injury to American women," "battering causes more injuries to women than car accidents, rapes, and muggings combined," or "25 to 35 percent of women in emergency rooms are there for injuries from domestic violence." These patently false numbers (data from the Justice Department and the Centers for Disease Control and Prevention suggest that less than 1 percent of women's emergency-room visits are due to assaults by male partners, and that about 10 times as many women are injured in auto accidents) are complemented by increasingly expansive definitions of abuse.

...

By 1982, largely due to lobbying by advocacy groups, a majority of states expanded police authority to make arrests in misdemeanor assaults which the officers had not actually witnessed—a move applauded by most law enforcement personnel and family violence researchers. But as the rate of arrest remained low, many states and jurisdictions began to go further and mandate arrests, a policy viewed with far more ambivalence. This trend has been boosted by the post-O.J. Simpson-trial attention to domestic abuse and by incentives for pro-arrest policies in the federal Violence Against Women Act of 1994.

...

The effects of mandatory arrest are compounded by no-drop prosecutions. The assumption behind no-drop policies is that when women recant or refuse to press charges, it is out of fear or dependence. But reality is far more complex. The woman may feel, rightly or not, that she is not in danger and can handle the situation better without the complications of a legal case; or the lines between aggressor and victim may be blurred; or the charge may have been false, made in anger, and later regretted.

...

Nowadays, however, some crusaders openly argue that domestic violence should be taken more seriously than other crimes. In 1996, the sponsor of a New York bill toughening penalties for misdemeanor assault on a family member (including ex-spouses and unwed partners) vowed to oppose a version extending the measure to all assaults: "The whole purpose of my bill is to single out domestic violence," Assemblyman Joseph Lentol said. "I don't want the world to think we're treating stranger assaults the same way as domestic assaults."

These arguments, however, are rooted in the paradigm of domestic violence promoted by the battered women's movement: The woman, powerless and trapped by economic or psychological dependency, is victimized by the brutal, domineering man who uses force to impose control. Certainly, some cases fit this model; but many others do not.

For one, the feminist paradigm ignores mutual combat and female aggression. Surveys by pioneering family violence researchers Murray Straus of the University of New Hampshire and Richard Gelles of the University of Rhode Island have found that half of all spousal violence is reciprocal while the rest is evenly split between female-only and male-only violence (though men are more likely to inflict serious damage). Those findings are confirmed by a host of other studies. Nonetheless, materials distributed by advocacy groups and used in training for judges, prosecutors, and police assert that

95 percent of domestic violence is male-on-female and dismiss mutual brawling as a "myth."

Because of this ideology, the War on Domestic Violence gets a bit schizophrenic when it comes to female aggression. Ironically, mandatory arrest laws have led to a rise in the number of women arrested for domestic assault, as sole perpetrators or together with their partners; in some states, women now account for about a quarter of all arrests. According to criminologist Lawrence Sherman, this "resulted in intensive lobbying [by battered women's advocates] not to arrest women regardless of probable cause to do so." In response, many jurisdictions have devised ways around formal gender neutrality.

...

While battered women's advocates have had a major impact on the ways in which charges of spousal assault are handled by criminal courts, the reach of the War on Domestic Violence is still somewhat limited by constitutional protections for defendants. Perhaps the worst excesses of this crusade are found in the use and abuse of civil orders of protection, also known as restraining orders—which require lower levels of evidence and can be issued without the accused having a chance to defend himself.

Court orders prohibiting one party not only from harassing but, in some cases, from approaching or contacting another are not limited to domestic violence cases. Normally, getting such an order is a cumbersome process. But under abuse prevention laws, on the books in 48 states by 1988, restraining orders are easily available against current or former spouses or cohabitants and some other family members.

...

Moreover, temporary restraining orders are granted ex parte, without the defendant being present or notified—much less informed of the specific charges. Supporters of current laws concede that getting an order takes very little evidence.

...

The consequences of a restraining order for the man on the receiving end (and it usually is a man) can be quite serious. If he shares a home with the plaintiff, he will usually be ordered to vacate the premises. Any contact becomes illegal—in many states, a felony punishable by prison or fines (it doesn't matter if the "victim" agreed to or even initiated the contact). This can have particularly wrenching consequences when there are children involved.

Men who have had restraining orders issued against them on the basis of uncorroborated or trivial allegations have been jailed for sending their kids a Christmas card; for asking a telephone operator to convey a harmless message; for accidental "contact" at the courthouse; and for returning a child's phone call.

...

Beyond questions of civil liberties and due process, there is no proof that the crackdown prevents domestic homicides, the ostensible goal of hardline restraining order procedures. Nor is there evidence that it prevents serious assaults. A man who intends to kill a woman and either plans to take his own life or knows that he will face murder charges won't be deterred by the penalties for violating a restraining order, as too many headlines show.

...

Indeed, it has become commonplace among lawyers of both sexes that restraining orders are routinely misused as a weapon in divorces. It's hard to come up with reliable estimates of how frequently that happens. But given the advantages conferred by a restraining order, from possession of the house to virtually automatic custody of the children, the temptation is certainly there.

...

Undoubtedly, there are cases in which victims of intimate violence are badly let down by the system, sometimes with fatal results. But apathy and excessive zeal can coexist—just as horror stories of children yanked from parental homes on flimsy suspicions of abuse coexist with ones of abused children handed back to their tormentors. Indeed, when apathy and excessive zeal do coexist, the policy implications are often disastrous.

...

Even if the dangerous cases are caught early, some people are going to be badly hurt or even killed by their mates. Such things are not always predictable. And we might ask, without creating a new "abuse excuse," whether being denied access to his children might not push a nonviolent person over the edge.

...

The most obvious casualties of the War on Domestic Violence have been men, particularly men involved in contentious divorces. But it has also hurt many of the women who are its intended beneficiaries. Part of the problem is the one-size-fits-all approach to domestic violence. For many couples in violent relationships, particularly those involved in mutual violence, joint counseling offers the best solution. But if they have come to the attention of the authorities, it's one form of counseling to which they are unlikely to be referred. Couples therapy is vehemently opposed by battered women's advocates—ostensibly out of concern for women's safety, but also because of the implication that both partners must change their behavior.

...

And then there are the women who, often on the basis of a misunderstanding or a single, trivial incident blown out of proportion, are labeled as victims against their will. "It was very paternalistic, even if women were involved in the system," says Susan Finkelstein, reflecting on her experience. "At one point, I told a prosecutor that I didn't appreciate being told what was best for me by someone who didn't even know me. She said, 'It strikes me as odd that you don't appreciate the fact that we're trying to protect you.' What I said didn't matter. It seems so ironic that in trying to give women a voice, they are taking away their voices."

Diana
Zuckerman
and Stacey
Friedman

Measuring the Cost of Domestic Violence against Women

Beginning in the late 1960s and early 1970s, the women's movement fought to reconceptualize domestic violence as a public issue rather than a private family problem. The success of this movement in bringing intimate violence to the attention of the public resulted in the passage of laws such as the Family Violence Prevention and Services Act of 1984 and the Violence Against Women Act of 1994. These laws have assisted victims by providing funding for services, brought more attention to issues of domestic violence, and led to efforts to collect data on the extent of domestic violence and to estimate its costs.

Defining Domestic Violence

The definition of domestic violence is a crucial element in determining its prevalence and calculating the associated costs, yet no consensus exists regarding the definition of domestic violence against women. While most prevalence estimates are calculated on the basis of physical violence in any intimate relationship, domestic violence is sometimes defined as a course of coercive conduct that includes physical force and/or a pattern of mental abuse and control including intense criticism, verbal harassment, sexual coercion and assaults, isolation due to restraint of normal activities and freedom, and denial of access to resources. Although this definition is important to our understanding of domestic violence, it is too complicated to use in most research studies. Domestic violence does not include child abuse or neglect, although children may be harmed by living in a home where domestic violence occurs, and there is a significant association between domestic violence and child abuse (Edleson, 1997a and 1997b). Moreover, domestic violence sometimes includes threatening a woman by threatening to harm her child or children.

Prevalence of Domestic Violence

A variety of national studies have attempted to document the prevalence of domestic violence against women, or the total number of cases in a given time period. Straus and Gelles (1986) found that the overall rate of husband-to-wife violence was 113 per 1,000 couples. Using a different survey, the Commonwealth Fund (1993) found that 84 of every 1,000 women living with or married to a man reported abuse in the last year. Although definitions of spouse abuse and domestic violence vary, research studies reviewed by Stark and Flitcraft (1991) and by Stout (1989) agree that approximately 20 percent of the adult female population are physically abused by a male intimate in their lifetime. Between 1992 and 1993, 29 percent of all acts of violence against women by a lone offender were committed by an intimate, defined as a husband, ex-husband, boyfriend, or ex-boyfriend (estimate based on National Crime Victimization Survey data; Bachman and Saltzman, 1995).

Direct and Indirect Costs

The economic costs of domestic violence can be categorized as two types—direct costs and indirect costs. Direct costs consist of the value of the goods and services used in treating or preventing domestic violence; indirect costs consist of the value of goods and services lost because of domestic violence.

Direct Costs

The Costs of Domestic Violence Project focused on the direct costs of domestic violence in the following areas:

- Health care, including emergency room care, hospitalization, initial or follow-up care at a clinic or doctor's office, nursing home care, dental care, mental health care, costs of treatment for sexually transmitted diseases, pregnancy complications and birth defects, and alcohol and drug abuse treatment;
- Child well-being, including child protective services, foster care, counseling, special education, teen pregnancy, and positive toxicology [drug addicted] infants;

- Housing, including emergency shelters for homeless and battered women, supported housing such as transitional, Section 8, or public housing, and foreclosure and eviction;
- Criminal justice and the legal system, including police time for arrests and responses to telephone calls, prison and detention costs, probation and parole costs, prosecution, criminal court, civil or family court, custody litigation, child support enforcement, and juvenile court;
- Social services, including domestic violence prevention/education, counseling, job training, advocacy program costs, training costs for police, doctors, etc.; and
- Other costs—for example, property damage.

Direct costs can be calculated by multiplying the prevalence of domestic violence by the cost of the services used as a result of the violence. This is a useful method for determining the cost-effectiveness of intervention strategies, because once a baseline cost is established, any change in the cost (either from a decline in prevalence or a decline in cost) from one year to the next can be evaluated after the implementation of a new intervention. Of course, not all interventions are successful in preventing future domestic violence.

Table 1 includes data on the prevalence of domestic violence in various services ("usage") and their costs. These data should be considered only as illustrative of how the cost model might be applied; costs vary in different regions of the country and services also vary widely. Further review is necessary before reliable total cost figures can be calculated.

Indirect Costs

In determining the indirect economic costs of domestic violence, the Costs of Domestic Violence Project focused on the following areas:

- Lost productivity, such as job loss and unemployment, productivity lost due to women prevented from working by her partner, coming in late or inability to concentrate due to violence at home, disruption at the workplace by the batterer, lost productivity at work for medical reasons, lost productivity at work for court appearances or other appointments, lost promotion/advancement, lost productivity due to incarceration, and lost productivity at home for medical or other reasons
- Mortality, including the death of the battered woman and, less frequently, the death of the batterer or their children
- Social and psychological costs, such as losses to women, communities and society in terms of quality of life and restraints on human

Table 1   Examples of Direct Costs of Domestic Violence

Service	Usage	Costs
Health care: Emergency room care	1.5 million women seek medical treatment for injuries related to abuse (AMA, 1992).	A study at Rush Medical Center in Chicago estimated an average charge for medical services to abused women, children, and older people as $1,633 per person per year, excluding psychological or follow-up costs (Meyer, 1992).
Child well-being: Foster care	Of the 256,000 children in foster care (1995 est.), an estimated 50% are victims of child abuse (Committee on Ways & Means, 1994). In 45–59% of child abuse cases, the mother is also being abused (McKibben, De Vos, & Newberger, 1989; Stark & Flitcraft, 1988). The percentage of child abuse or foster care cases that result from domestic violence is unknown.	$2.5 billion federal foster care expenditures under Title IV-E in 1993 (Committee on Ways & Means, 1994). New York spends $13,600 per child per year in foster care benefits, excluding protective services (Zorza, 1994).
Homelessness: Emergency shelters	41% of homeless women in family shelters report that they had been battered (Bassuk & Rosenberg, 1988).	The Women Against Abuse Center in Philadelphia reported an annual budget of $2.5 million, or $68 per person per day for housing and services (*Working Woman*, 1994).
Criminal justice: Prison and detention costs of batterers	20,170 male prisoners were incarcerated for harming an intimate in 1991 (U.S. DOJ, 1994).	Average annual operating expenditures per inmate for all state and federal correctional facilities (nationwide) in 1990 were $15,513 (U.S. DOJ, 1992).

Note: For a more complete description of the full range of indirect costs, see the full report.

potential and activities. Indicators for measuring such costs are in their infancy and are therefore excluded from the indirect economic costs model in the Costs of Domestic Violence Project. However, some of the potential indirect social and psychological costs are discussed below.

Lost Productivity and Mortality   In determining the indirect economic cost of domestic violence, researchers need to consider two kinds of values: (1) the cost of lost productivity (e.g., from illness, court appearances, or incarceration), and (2) the cost of mortality. Much of the data on productivity losses is based on small-scale studies, and data on the prevalence of domestic violence among working women are not available. Nevertheless, preliminary calculations for losses due to domestic violence can be made. Table 2 demonstrates how we can integrate the finding that 30 percent of abused working women lose their jobs with information on women's earnings by age to yield estimates of the cost of lost productivity.

The Need for Further Research

To our knowledge, there are no national studies that determine the direct costs of domestic violence against women; no national studies to determine the extent of the lost productivity for employers, households, and communities from this source of violence against women; and insufficient data to assess the effectiveness of family violence services in reducing the prevalence of abuse. Domestic violence against women is a legitimate social problem requiring

Table 2   Examples of Indirect Costs

Cause	Number Affected
Job loss of victim	24–30% of abused working women reported losing their jobs (Shepard & Pence, 1988; Stanley, 1992).
Poor work habits	64% of battered women arrive at work an hour late 5 times per month (Stanley, 1992).
Disruption at workplace	75% of victims are harassed at work by abuser (Friedman & Couper, 1987).
Lost productivity due to premature mortality	29% of female homicide victims are murdered by an intimate or other relative (Bachman & Saltzman, 1995).

substantial investment by the public and private sectors. Credible information about the number of individuals affected and the economic cost to victims, institutions, taxpayers, and society will be useful in generating support for that investment. Without such information, policymakers, taxpayers, foundations, private firms, and the medical, criminal justice, and social service establishments will likely be unwilling to allocate increasingly scarce resources to address this problem.

KEY WEBSITES

STALKING AND DOMESTIC VIOLENCE: THE THIRD ANNUAL REPORT TO CONGRESS UNDER THE VIOLENCE AGAINST WOMEN ACT

This annual report to Congress is part of an ongoing program to share information about strategies that show promise in the field and research that enhances our understanding of stalking and domestic violence. It is produced in response to Subtitle F of the Violence Against Women Act, which directs the attorney general to submit an annual report on these issues.
http://www.ojp.usdoj.gov/vawgo/stalk98

CITATIONS ON DOMESTIC OCCURRENCE OF SPOUSAL ABUSE

This site provides an extensive list of citations with summaries of research, journal articles, and books.
http://www.acfc.org/study/dom-viol.htm

U.S. DEPARTMENT OF JUSTICE: THE VIOLENCE AGAINST WOMEN GRANTS OFFICE

The Violence Against Women Grants Office (VAWGO) in the Office of Justice Programs (OJP) is dedicated to enhancing victim safety and ensuring offender accountability by supporting policies, protocols, and projects that call for zero tolerance of all forms of violence against women, including domestic violence, sexual assault, and stalking. The site includes links to a variety of government reports on domestic violence and abuse of women.
http://www.ojp.usdoj.gov/vawgoreports.htm

NATIONAL INSTITUTE OF JUSTICE RESEARCH REPORT— THE CRIMINALIZATION OF DOMESTIC VIOLENCE: PROMISES AND LIMITS

Jeffrey Fagan, *National Institute of Justice Research Report—The Criminalization of Domestic Violence: Promises and Limits*: Research on arrest and prosecution, civil or criminal protection orders, batterer treatment, and community interventions has generated weak or inconsistent evidence of deterrent effects on either repeat victimization or repeat offending. Fagan notes that for every study that shows promising results, one or more show either no effect or even negative results that increase the risks to victims. This report discusses the factors to consider when implementing programs.
http://www.ncjrs.org/txtfiles/crimdom.txt
or
http://www.ncjrs.org/pdffiles/crimdom.pdf

HUSBAND BATTERING

The philosophy behind this site is that husband abuse should not be viewed as merely the opposite side of the coin to wife abuse. Both are part of the same problem, which should be described as one *person* abusing another *person*. The problem should not be seen as a gender issue. The site includes an extensive list of links to articles, citations with commentary, homicide rates, bibliographies, case histories, and personal testimony.

http://www.vix.com/pub/men/battery/battery.html

GAY AND LESBIAN DOMESTIC VIOLENCE

Laws written to address domestic violence from a heterosexual perspective can make it difficult for a battered lesbian, gay man, bisexual, or transgendered person to escape the cycle of abuse that is characteristic of domestic violence. For a victim of abuse by a partner of the same sex, restraining orders and other protections may be difficult to obtain. This site presents a great deal of information about this issue.

http://www.web.apc.org/~jharnick/violence.html

NATIONAL COALITION AGAINST SEXUAL ASSAULT

The National Coalition Against Sexual Assault is a feminist organization that provides leadership to the movement to end sexual violence. It does this through advocacy, education, and public policy.

http://www.ncasa.org

THE STRUCTURE OF FAMILY VIOLENCE: AN ANALYSIS OF SELECTED INCIDENTS (FEDERAL BUREAU OF INVESTIGATION/UNIFORM CRIME REPORTS)

This site provides an empirical examination of family violence in the United States. A family violence incident is defined as one that includes the existence of at least one relationship between the victim and the offender that is within the family. The offenses discussed include murder and nonnegligent homicide, forcible rape, stalking, intimidation, robbery, aggravated assault, and simple assault, among others.

http://www.fbi.gov/ucr/nibrs/famvio21.pdf

Are Stepfamilies Destined for Trouble?

Throughout history, the reputation of stepfamilies has been surprisingly negative. The general thinking has been that the stepchild suffers in such families and that the suffering is caused by the stepmother. The stepmother has come down to us as a figure of cruelty and evil, constantly plotting to harm her stepchildren in a variety of ways. Just think of the Cinderella or Snow White fairy tales. The French word *maratre* means both "stepmother" and "a cruel and harsh mother." In English literature, the word "stepmother" is often preceded by "wicked." The stepchild was often a child who did not belong or whose status was similar to that of an orphan. In fact, "stepchild" originally meant "orphan."

Much of this has changed today, and stepfamilies have become a common sight on the American family landscape. The United States has the highest incidence of stepfamilies in the world. It is estimated that about 17 percent of married-couple households involve a stepparent. About one child in six is a stepchild.

The stepfamilies of today are different from those of the past in how they have come into being. The vast majority of stepfamilies now come about because of the marriage or cohabitation of mothers and fathers of children whose other parent is still living. Of these, the largest group by far is composed of families formed by the remarriage of divorced men and women. The high divorce rate is the key factor in the rise of the modern stepfamily.

In the past, stepfamilies resulted from quite different conditions and had different implications. Usually they were the product of remarriage after the death of a spouse. Mortality and the frequency of remarriage by the widowed determined the number of stepfamilies. Moreover, unlike today, children who lived in stepfamilies rarely had more than one living parent. In the past, a stepparent usually replaced a deceased parent. Today, a stepparent is often an additional parent figure that a child must incorporate.

A stepparent must enter a family system that has been created by the custodial parent and her children. The new marriage partners must establish their own relationship in an existing family structure. They must create new rules for how the family is to be run. Such changes may produce disadvantages or tensions among the family members.

Are the difficulties such new families must overcome a prescription for trouble? Andrew J. Cherlin and Frank F. Furstenberg Jr., in their article "Stepfamilies in the United States: A Reconsideration," contend that they are, because these families must overcome a variety of problems. Remarriage makes parenthood and kinship an achieved status rather than an ascribed status. Traditionally a person became a father or a mother at the birth of a child. One did not have to do anything else to be a parent, nor could one easily resign from the job, especially in a family system that strongly discouraged divorce.

Remarriage after divorce, though, adds a number of other potential kinship positions. The new parent must now achieve the status of parent or some other role that may resemble it. Working out these arrangements presents many more problems than are usually encountered in a first-marriage family.

Virginia Rutter, in her essay "Lessons from Stepfamilies," notes that although second marriages are less stable than first ones—with a breakup rate of 60 percent versus 50 percent for first marriages—that statistic conceals the very real success of stepfamilies. She points out that stepfamilies do indeed face instability, but that the shakiness occurs early in the marriage—and may ultimately be traced to a lack of support from the culture. When the culture is slow to view them as a "real family," their chances of success are undermined. Nevertheless, Rutter believes that once stepfamilies make it over the early hurdles, they are even stronger than traditional families. She thinks second marriages may certainly be more complex than first-marriage families—but they are also richer.

Yes

Stepfamilies in the United States: A Reconsideration

Andrew J.
Cherlin and
Frank F.
Furstenberg Jr.

...

Among developed nations, the United States has unusually high rates of divorce and remarriage. Close to a third of all Americans will marry, divorce, and remarry.

...

One of the taken-for-granted aspects of family life in the West has been that the parents and children in the conjugal family will live in the same household until the children grow up. Until the last few decades, that assumption was justified. The increases, first, in divorce and remarriage and, more recently, in cohabitation and out-of-wedlock childbearing, have made this assumption problematic.... Divorce splits the conjugal family into two households—one that typically contains a custodial parent (usually the mother) and the children and a second that contains the noncustodial parent (usually the father).

Remarriage can bring a multitude of ties across households, creating what one of us has called "the new extended family" (Furstenberg, 1987).

...

How are we to make sense of this admixture? How many families are involved? What are their boundaries? The relationships spill over the sides of households, with children providing the links from one to the next.... [I]n developed Western societies, we are accustomed to thinking of immediate families as being contained within households. We define a stepfamily household as a household that contains a parent with children from a previous union

From *Annual Review of Sociology* 20 (January 1, 1994). Copyright © 1994 by Annual Reviews. Reprinted with permission. www.AnnualReviews.org

and that parent's current partner. The children from the previous union are the stepchildren, and the current partner is the stepparent. The household can be even more complex: Both partners may have children from previous unions and they also may have a new, mutual child from the current union. But the defining criterion is that they all reside in the same household.

...

Doing the Work of Kinship

When Americans think about kinship, they tend to think about people related through either "blood" or marriage (Schneider, 1980). Mere existence of a blood tie, however, does not necessarily make two people think of each other as kin. Kinship is achieved by establishing a "relationship," seeing each other regularly, corresponding, giving or receiving help—that is, by making repeated connections. The absence of a relationship may mean that even a blood relative may not be counted as family. To be sure, almost everyone considers their parents and their children to be kin even if they have not seen them in a long time. But Americans would understand what someone meant if she said, "My father left home when I was three and I never saw him again; he's not part of my family. My stepfather is really the person I consider to be my father." And similarly a person might not regard a cousin as a relative if he never met her.

To be a relative, you must do the work of creating and maintaining kinship. Among parents and children, this happens almost automatically—so much so that we rarely think about it. But among stepparents and stepchildren it does not happen automatically. For one thing, a stepparent in a remarriage that has followed a divorce does not replace the stepchild's nonresident parent, as was the case when most remarriages followed a death.... Rather, the stepparent adds to the stepchild's stock of potential kin. If both biological parents are still involved in the stepchild's life, it is not clear what role the stepparent is supposed to play. There are few guidelines, few norms. This situation is what led one of us to conclude that the role of the stepparent is incompletely institutionalized (Cherlin, 1978).

In fact, there is great variability in how stepparents and stepchildren view each other. In a ... national survey, children ages 11 to 16 and their parents both were asked who they specifically included in their family. Although only 1 percent of parents did not mention their biological children, 15 percent of those with stepchildren in the household did not mention them. Among children, 31 percent of those in stepfamily households omitted the stepparent who was living with them, and 41 percent failed to mention a stepsibling (Furstenberg, 1987).

What, then, determines how stepchildren and stepparents view each other? A key factor is how old the child was when the stepparent joined the household: The younger the child, the more likely he or she is to consider the stepparent to be a "real" parent (Marsiglio, 1992). The evidence isn't precise enough to establish an age cutoff for emotional bonding. Still, we suspect that if the stepparent arrives during the preschool years (before the child is five), it is possible to establish a parent-like relationship; but if the stepparent arrives much later, strong bonds form much more rarely. Research shows that children establish strong bonds of attachment to their parents, whom they rely on for security, within their first year or two.

...

The kinship terms used by children to designate their parents are one measure of the bonding process. There is no agreed-upon direct term of reference for a stepparent (Cherlin, 1978). For example, few if any children call their stepfather "Step-Dad," and it would be equally rare for children to refer to him formally as "Mr. Jones." Instead, some will call him "Dad" but many will use the stepparent's first name. In the absence of empirical research that relates the use of terminology to bonding, we are inclined to think that the use of the first name suggests a relationship that is neither parent nor stranger, but somewhere in between. If children do not address stepparents using the parental term for the biological parent, then children may not grant stepparents the reciprocal rights and obligations ordinarily accorded to so-called "real" parents.

...

In other words, remarriage is making parenthood and kinship an achieved status rather than an ascribed status, to use the classic distinction in anthropology and sociology (Davis, 1948; Eisenstadt, 1966). Traditionally, being a father or a mother had been a status ascribed to individuals at the birth of their child, which generally occurred only after the couple married. To be sure, people marry and have children through their own efforts; nevertheless, one did not have to do anything else to be a parent, nor could one easily resign from the job, especially in a family system that strongly discouraged divorce. In this sort of stable family system, being a grandparent was similarly ascribed. Those rules still apply to the majority of children who are born to two married parents.

Remarriage after divorce, though, adds a number of other, potential kinship positions. Whether these positions are filled depends on the actions of the individuals involved. The most obvious positions are stepfather and stepmother. We have discussed the wide variation in the roles that stepparents play. Some are parent-like figures who are intensely involved with their stepchildren. Many others are more like friends or uncles and aunts. Others, particularly stepparents who don't live with their stepchildren every day, may be like distant cousins—available for a kinship relation but, in fact, rarely assuming an important position in the child's network. In all cases, how much like a family member a stepparent becomes depends directly on his or her efforts to develop a close relationship with stepchildren. Kinship relations in stepfamilies belong to the broader category of in-law relationships—ties created by marriage or marriage-like arrangements. Such ties are characteristically discretionary and even more so in the absence of marriage.

···

Stepfamily "Process": Building a Stepfamily

After divorce, single parents and their children establish, often with some difficulty, agreed-upon rules and new daily schedules. They establish ways of relating to each other that may differ from the pre-disruption days. A daughter may become a special confidante to her mother. A son may take out the garbage, wash the car, and perform other tasks his father used to do. Put another way, single parents and children create a new family system. Then, into that system, with its shared history, intensive relationships, and agreed-upon roles, walks a stepparent. It can be difficult for the members of the stepfamily household to adjust to his or her presence.

Recent research suggests that the adjustment can take years to complete. One family therapist argues that the average stepfamily takes about seven years to finish the process (Papernow, 1988). That is a long time, considering that more than one-fourth of all remarriages disrupt within five years (Martin and Bumpass, 1989). At the start, the stepparent is an outsider, almost an intruder in the system. At first, the stepparent may view himself naively as a healer who will nurse the wounded family back to health (Papernow, 1988). But his initial efforts may hurt rather than help him attain his goal: A stepdaughter may resent the intimacy and support a new stepfather provides to her mother; a son may not wish to relinquish washing the car to a well-meaning stepfather who thinks he is just doing what fathers are supposed to do. As the two of us wrote, "stepparents quickly discover that they have been issued only a limited license to parent." The wiser ones among them accept the limits of their job description and wait for their time to arrive (Furstenberg and Cherlin, 1991: 85).

According to recent articles, family therapists seem to agree that for a stepfamily household to be successful, the remarried couple must build a boundary around themselves and work together to solve problems. This process is made more complicated by the negative images of stepparents in the larger culture (Ganong et al., 1990) and their weak status in our legal system (Fine and Fine, 1992).

···

During this process of family building, research suggests, it can be harder to be a stepmother than a stepfather (White, 1993). In the typical remarriage chain, the children live with their biological mother and a stepfather; they visit their biological father and his new wife, who is their stepmother. Consequently, the typical stepmother does not live with her stepchildren; rather, she must establish a relationship during the visits. She usually is seeing children whose primary tie is to their biological mother, with whom she must compete. In contrast, stepfathers compete with non-custodial fathers, many of whom see little of their children (Seltzer, 1991). Moreover, in the minority of cases in which the children live with the step-mother and the biological father, other difficulties can arise. In these atypical cases, the children may have been subject to a custody battle, or they may have been sent to live with the father because the mother could not control their behavior (Ihinger-Tallman and Pasley, 1987). And mothers who are noncustodial parents visit their children and telephone them more often than do noncustodial fathers, creating competition with the stepmother (Furstenberg and Nord, 1985; White, 1993).

Stepfathers, in other words, often can fill a vacuum left by the departed biological father. Stepmothers, in contrast, must inhabit the space already occupied by the biological mother. Moreover, stepmothers may judge themselves according to the culturally dominant view that mothers should play the major role in rearing children; if so, they may fall short of these high standards. Stepfathers, in contrast, may hold themselves to the lower standard, namely, that fathers are supposed to provide support to the mother but let her do most of the hands-on child rearing. If so, they may feel satisfied with their role performance, even if they are doing less than many dissatisfied stepmothers (Keshet, 1988; White, 1993).

One critical area of family building that has not received much attention is the merging of economic systems. Of course, nuclear families must integrate economic resources and devise a system of allocating funds. Still, it is obvious that divorce complicates this process.... Also, there are the inevitable problems of dividing the expenses of child rearing between current and former partners.

...

Effects on Children

Fifteen years ago, the two of us thought that remarriage would improve the overall well-being of children whose parents had divorced. For one thing, when a single mother remarries, her household income usually rises dramatically because men's wages are so much higher, on average, than are women's wages. One national study found that 8 percent of children in mother-stepfather households were living below the poverty line, compared to 49 percent of children in single-mother households (Bachrach, 1983). Consequently, if a divorce causes a decline in household income that hurts the well-being of children, then an increase in household income after the mother remarries should improve children's well-being. In addition, the stepparent adds a second adult to the home. He or she can provide support to the custodial parent and reinforce the custodial parent's monitoring and control of the children's behavior. A stepparent also can provide an adult role model for a child of the same gender.

Despite these advantages, many studies now show that the well-being of children in stepfamily households is no better, on average, than the well-being of children in divorced, single-parent households. Both groups of children show lower levels of well-being than do children in two-biological-parent families.

...

A national health survey of 15,000 children ... produced similar results. Children in stepfamily households and in single-parent households both received higher average scores on a checklist of behavior problems than did children in nondivorced, two-parent households. When parents were asked questions about the need for psychological help for their children, 3 percent of nondivorced parents said that their child needed help or had received help in the previous year, compared to 10 percent in single-mother households and 10 percent in mother-stepfather households. Both of the latter groups had children who were more likely to have repeated a grade in school than did children from nondivorced households. On all of these indicators, there was little difference between the children in single-parent households and in stepfamily households (Zill, 1988).

There is conflicting evidence as to whether children of different ages or genders adjust differently to the arrival of a stepparent. Several studies, conducted mostly with younger children, have found that girls had a more difficult time adjusting to the presence of a stepfather than boys did adjusting to a stepmother (Bray, 1988; Hetherington, 1987). Some of the authors speculated that girls tend to form close bonds to their divorced mothers and that these bonds are disrupted by the arrival of a stepfather. In support of this idea, at least two studies found that daughters showed poorer adjustment when their mothers and stepfathers reported greater cohesion and bonding in their marriage; conversely, they showed better adjustment when there was less cohesion in the marriage (Brand et al., 1988; Bray, 1988). It is as if the daughters' sense of well-being falls at least temporarily when their mothers turn some attention and affection toward their new husbands.

...

Only one finding is well-established concerning the long-term effects on children of having lived in a stepfamily household. Children in stepfamily households—particularly girls—leave their households at an earlier age than do children in single-parent households or in two-parent households. They leave earlier to marry; and they also leave earlier to establish independent households prior to marrying. An analysis of a large, six-year, national study of high school students showed this pattern for girls (Goldscheider and Goldscheider, 1993).

...

[A] national sample of currently married persons suggested that tensions between stepchildren and their parents and stepparents cause the early home-leaving. Those who had stepchildren in their households reported more family problems involving children. The authors hypothesize that one way these problems are resolved is by encouraging, or arranging for, the stepchildren to leave the household.

···

It is important to recognize that some stepparents manage to build relations with their partner's children, though rarely so if their remarriage dissolves. Still, the odds of building durable and intimate bonds that resemble the strong ties that often occur among biological parents and children are relatively low. The discretionary quality of in-law relationships—especially relationships that have a legacy of conflict or emotional distance—often seems to dictate the kinship bonds in later life.

···

Of course, we are aware that multiple parent-figures complicate both the legal system and the parenting system. But the idea that two parents per household is the standard and the only acceptable family form is giving way to a more diverse set of family arrangements that are not so neatly confined to a single household. The change in family forms that we have been tracing introduces a host of anomalies. We see little evidence that remarriage (formal and informal) has become more institutionalized since the two of us first began to write about this growing phenomenon. We see some troubling indications that the cultural, legal, and social anomalies associated with "recycling the family" place a considerable burden on a growing number of children—even if most children seem capable of managing that burden without serious effects.

Lessons from Stepfamilies

**Virginia
Rutter**

Here we are, three decades into the divorce revolution, and we still don't quite know what to make of stepfamilies. We loved the Brady Bunch, but that was before we discovered how unreal they were. Now that stepfamilies embrace one of three children and, one way or another, impact the vast majority of Americans, we can't seem to get past seeing them as the spawn of failure, the shadow side of our overidealized traditional family. When we think of them at all, we see only what they are not—hence their designation as "nontraditional" families, female headed households and unwed moms, gay parents, and other permutations that make up the majority of families today.

...

Despite their ambiguous standing, stepfamilies are getting first-class attention from social scientists. Much of what they are discovering is eye-opening. Although, for example, it is widely known that second marriages are less stable than first ones—with a breakup rate of 60 percent, versus 50 percent for first marriages—that statistic paints stepfamilies with too broad a brush; it conceals their very real success. A far more useful, more important fact is that stepfamilies do indeed face instability, but that shakiness occurs early in the remarriage—and may ultimately be traced to lack of support from the culture. In denying them the status of a "real family," we may be doing much to undermine their chances of success. Nevertheless, once remarriage families make it over the early hurdle, they are even stronger than traditional families.

Let this turnabout truth serve as a metaphor for what is now coming to light about stepfamilies. They are certainly more complex than first-marriage families—but they are also richer. New information about what really goes on, and what goes wrong, in stepfamilies will definitely change the way you think about them. It also promises to change the way you think about all families. Among the new findings:

- Contrary to myth, stepfamilies have a high rate of success in raising healthy children. Eighty percent of the kids come out fine.

- These stepkids are resilient, and a movement to study their resilience—not just their problems—promises to help more kids succeed in any kind of family, traditional or otherwise.

- What trips stepkids up has little to do with stepfamilies per se. The biggest source of problems for kids in stepfamilies is parental conflict left over from the first marriage.

- A detailed understanding of the specific problems stepfamilies encounter now exists, courtesy of longitudinal research—not studies that tap just the first six months of stepfamily adjustment.

- Stepfamilies turn out to be a gender trap—expectations about women's roles and responsibilities are at the root of many problems that develop in stepfamilies.

- After five years, stepfamilies are more stable than first-marriage families, because second marriages are happier than first marriages. Stepfamilies experience most of their troubles in the first two years.

- Stepfamilies are not just make-do households limping along after loss. All members experience real gains, notably the opportunity to thrive under a happier relationship.

- The needs of people in stepfamilies are the needs of people in all families—to be accepted, loved, and cared about; to maintain attachments; to belong to a group and not be a stranger; and to feel some control by maintaining order in their lives. It's just that these needs are made acutely visible—and unavoidable—in stepfamilies.

The Myths and the Research

Despite the prevalence of stepfamilies, myths about them abound. You probably know some of them: There's an Evil Stepmother, mean, manipulative, and jealous. The stepfather is a molester, a sexual suspect.... The ex-wife is victimized, vindictive, interfering—a She-Devil. The ex-husband is withdrawn, inept, the contemporary Absentee Father. And the kids are nuisances intent on ruining their parents' lives; like Maisie in Henry James's story of nineteenth century postdivorce life, they play the parents and stepparents like billiard balls.

... Stepfamilies are a challenge. There are attachments that must be maintained through a web of conflicting emotions. There are ambiguities of identity, especially in the first years. Adults entering stepfamilies rightly feel anxious about their performance in multiple roles (spouse, instant parent) and about their acceptance by the kids and by the ex-spouse, who must remain a caring parent to the children. When an ex-spouse's children become someone else's stepchildren and spend time in a "stranger's" home, he or she worries about the children's comfort, their role models—and their loyalty.

Out of this worry are born the mythic stereotypes—and the fear of reliving a bad fairy tale. A stepmother, for example, forced to take on the role of disciplinarian because the children's biological father may lack a clear understanding of his own responsibilities, is set up to be cast as evil.

Still, there is a growing recognition among researchers that for every real pitfall a myth is built on, stepfamilies offer a positive opportunity in return.

...

It is now clear from detailed research that the adaptation to stepfamily relationships depends on the timing of the transition in the children's lives, the individuals involved, and the unique changes and stresses presented to the group.

The 80 Percent Who Succeed

Hetherington and Bray (1993) found that children in postdivorce and remarriage families may experience depression, conduct disorders, lower academic performance, and delinquency. Such problems are the result of reductions in parental attention that may immediately follow divorce or remarriage. There are the distractions of starting a new marriage. Such lapses may also be the outgrowth of parental conflict. They may reflect a noncustodial parent's withdrawal from the scene altogether. There's the stress of reductions in resources—typically, the lowered income of divorced mothers—and the disruption of routines, so highly valued by children, when two residences are established.

[H]owever, 80 percent of children of divorce and remarriage do not have behavior problems, despite the expectations and challenges, compared to 90 percent of children of first-marriage families. Kids whose parents divorce and remarry are not doomed.

This high success rate ... is a testament to the resilience of children. Further study, [the researchers] believe, can teach us more about the strengths summoned up in stepfamilies—and how to support them. But that would also contradict the gloom-and-doom scenarios that, though they do not actually describe most stepfamilies, often get trotted out on state occasions.

...

The Corporating Factor

It turns out that it's the parents, not the stepfamily, that make the most difference in the success of stepfamilies.

...

Today's most familiar stepfamily setup is a mother and her biological children living with a man who is not their birth father, and a noncustodial father in another residence—although the dilemmas of maintaining parenting responsibilities are much more complicated than who lives with whom. The U.S. Bureau of the Census reports that 14 percent of children in stepfamilies live with their biological father, 86 percent live with their biological mother and their stepfather. Whatever the situation, the parents' job is to find a way to stay in touch with each other so that both can remain completely in touch with their children.

Study after study shows that divorce and remarriage do not harm children—parental conflict does. That was the conclusion of research psychologist Robert Emery, Ph.D., of the University of Virginia, and Rex Forehand, Ph.D., of the University of Georgia, in a 1993 review of the divorce research. Sociologist Andrew Cherlin, Ph.D., author of the classic *Divided Families*, reported in *Science* magazine that children with difficulty after divorce started having problems long before divorce took place, as a result of parental conflict.

While divorce forces temporary disruption and a period of adjustment to loss and to new routines, marital conflict produces long-term disturbances. Depression and anger, often acted out in behavior problems, substance abuse, and delinquency, are all especially common among children in families where conflict rages. Following divorce, adversarial coparenting or the withdrawal of one of the parents from his or her (but usually his) role undermines children's healthy development.

The solution, of course, is cooperation of the parents in coparenting following divorce and remarriage. Desirable as it is, cooperative parenting between divorced spouses is rare, attained only in a minority of cases, Hetherington and Bray note.

Why Is Coparenting So Difficult?

Most marriages don't end mutually with friendship—so jealousy and animosity are easily aroused—and ex-spouses aren't two folks practiced at getting along anyway. Yet the ability of exes to get along is a key to the success of a new stepfamily.

Remarriage of one or both ex-spouses only enlarges the challenge of getting along—while possibly increasing tension between the ex-spouses responsible for coparenting. A stepparent who becomes a part of the kids' lives usually has no relationship to the child's other biological parent; if anything there is hostility.

...

If coparenting can be accomplished, children benefit in at least two ways. They feel loved by both biological parents; no child can thrive without affectionate connections. And they gain from being exposed to remarried adults in a successful intimate relationship. Especially when remarriage occurs before the children are teenagers, there is great potential for easy adaptation and smooth development.

A remarriage at adolescence, however, poses added challenges to the adjustment and success of the stepfamily, Hetherington and Bray report. It's a critical time of identity formation. Daughters are particularly apt to get into fights with a stepmother. Sexual tension may develop between a stepfather and a budding adolescent stepdaughter, made manifest in aloofness and what every parent knows as snottiness. Even if the divorce occurred many years before, a parent's remarriage during a child's teen years can revive adjustment difficulties that may have cropped up during the divorce.

Generally, though, a successful second marriage helps to reduce—if not eliminate—kids' problems. Divorced people are generally more compatible with their second partner than their first—even though there is a higher divorce rate among second marriages.

...

Looking at the Problems

While stepfamilies are doing a lot better than they're generally given credit for, a not insubstantial 20 percent of them—or twice the number of first-marriage families—do have problems with the kids. The research illuminating the specific problems in stepfamilies points to the basic requirements of stepfamilies as the major stumbling blocks. Cooperative coparenting. Equal involvement of both parents after the divorce. Noninterference by stepparents. Support for the coparenting relationship.

...

During the early months of remarriage, behavior problems rise steeply among the children. This is a time when stepfamilies are not yet cohesive—they are not likely to think of themselves as a unit. Gradually, behavior problems subside over the next two years. By then stepfamilies are just as likely as first-marriage families to have developed useful ways of communicating, rules of behavior, and discipline. They may not consider themselves as cohesive, but objective evaluation finds few practical differences.

... [T]rouble with the children developed when there was a reduction in time and attention from one or both parents, and reduced resources.

...

But even the reduced parental attention does not doom the children. Hetherington and Bray observe that the reduced parental attention can also be seen as an opportunity for the children to take on responsibility. The end result is that some children—almost always daughters—wind up more capable and competent.

...

One of the sizable traps in remarriage is the temptation a new spouse may feel to interfere with the coparenting process.... The new spouse may feel insecure or jealous of the coparent's continuing attachment to the former spouse. Still, that only succeeds in dividing the loyalty of the biological parent. A weekly conversation with an ex-spouse about the kids might trouble an anxious new spouse—but the communication is essential and the stepparent has the obligation to adjust, just as the parents do, for the good of the kids.

The Ultimate Trap

Name a stepfamily dilemma and women—biomothers, stepmothers, even stepdaughters—are at the center of the problem. Psychologists know that women are always more likely to express distress wherever troubles exist. But stepfamilies are the ultimate gender trap. Ever sensitive to interpersonal problems, women sense problems all over the place in stepfamilies.

Traditional male and female roles are troublesome enough, for the marriage and the children, in first-marriage families. But they wreak havoc on stepfamilies, Carter explains; they don't work at all. Indeed, researchers report that there's more equality in the marriage and in the distribution of domestic tasks in stepfamilies. But they still have a lot to learn—or unlearn—about gender roles and domestic life.

"No matter what we say or how feminist you are, everybody knows that women take care of children and men bring in most of the money. This sucks the stepmother into a quagmire of traditional domestic roles; it's not only that somebody makes her do it, she also does it to herself," explains Carter, coauthor of *The Invisible Web: Gender Patterns in Family Relationships*.

...

The Myth of the Happy Family

If stepfamilies make it out of the gender trap, there's one more to avoid—the myth of the nuclear family. Successful stepfamilies let go of their fantasy of a traditional family life, reports James Bray. They become more realistic, less romantic, and more flexible about family. They can cope with what life deals.

But remarriage often sets up conditions pulling the other way. "There's often a sense of defensiveness," explains Betty Carter. "There's a feeling of 'Let's not rock the boat this time. Let's be a happy family immediately so we can prove that this complicated thing—the divorce, the new marriage—was the right move.' People try to achieve an instant family, they don't allow for disgruntlement, fear, anxiety. Now we know it takes about five years for a stepfamily to become fully integrated."

Carter advises stepfamilies to "kiss the nuclear family good-bye. Stepfamilies simply cannot draw a tight circle around the household in the same way that nuclear families do. That always excludes somebody." The stepfamily's task is to keep permeable boundaries around the household, to facilitate coparenting, and to allow children access to the noncustodial parent.

It's a lot like tightrope-walking. "At the very time a stepfamily is trying to achieve its own integration, it has to keep the doors wide open and stay in touch with another household. You are not the lord of all you survey, as in the traditional family myth. You are on the phone regularly with someone about whom you feel, at best, ambivalent."

...

Many stepfamilies who start off using step terminology eventually drop it all, reports James Bray. It may be the surest sign of integration. The terms "stepmother" and "stepfather" help clarify roles and remind everybody who belongs to whom, and under what terms, in the transition. Later, though, they don't bother with such names. "Labels connote a struggle for identity that doesn't exist anymore for these groups," says Bray.

...

The naming issue underscores what stepfamilies have that original families don't always get: There is no monolithic view of what a stepfamily is supposed to be, or even be called. To catalog stepfamily experiences would be to catalog all relationships—there is endless variety, and unlimited routes to success or failure. Unlike traditional families, stepfamilies allow much more room for diversity. And equality. Count that as the ultimate lesson from stepfamilies.

KEY WEBSITES

STEPFAMILY ASSOCIATION OF AMERICA

The Stepfamily Association of America provides information, education, and advocacy for stepfamilies and those who work with them. It develops and disseminates research-based information and materials; designs, implements, and evaluates educational opportunities; evaluates and recommends materials, programs, and standards of practice; and advocates for financial, institutional, political, and social changes that support stepfamilies.
http://www.stepfam.org

NON-CUSTODIAL PARENTS' PARTICIPATION IN THEIR CHILDREN'S LIVES: EVIDENCE FROM THE SURVEY OF INCOME AND PROGRAM PARTICIPATION

Christine Winquist Nord and Nicholas Zill, "Non-Custodial Parents' Participation in Their Children's Lives: Evidence from the Survey of Income and Program Participation, Volume II: Final Report." (Prepared for the Office of Human Services Policy, Office of the Assistant Secretary for Planning and Evaluation, U.S. Department of Health and Human Services, August 14, 1996.): The aim of this project was to improve understanding of the relationship between noncustodial parent involvement, children's well-being, child support, and custody arrangements. The report contains an extensive literature review, selected annotated articles, and an extended bibliography.
http://www.acfc.org/study/dhhsvol2.htm

NON-CUSTODIAL PARENT'S PARTICIPATION IN THEIR CHILDREN'S LIVES

A nonresidential parent often becomes detached over time, paying minimal or no child support and visiting infrequently if at all. The costs to the children involved and to society at large of this disengagement are far from trivial. Many noncustodial parents do not pay all the child support they owe. Many others have no obligation to pay support. The aim of this project was to improve understanding of the relationship between noncustodial parent involvement, children's well-being, child support, and custody arrangements.
http://aspe.hhs.gov/fathers/sipp/xsnoncus.htm

EXPLAINING PSYCHOLOGICAL DISTRESS IN A SAMPLE OF REMARRIED AND DIVORCED PERSONS

Adam D. Shapiro, University of Texas at Austin, Department of Sociology, "Explaining Psychological Distress in a Sample of Remarried and Divorced Persons: The Influence of Economic Distress": Considerable research has been conducted during the past 25 years on the relationship between marriage and mental health. This study uses a large national data set to examine how financial resources influence the psychological distress levels of men and women who remarry following divorce.

http://www.unf.edu/~ashapiro/jfi.htm

TYPICAL STEPFAMILIES ARE NOT LIKE INTACT BIOFAMILIES!

Peter K. Gerlach, MSW, "Typical Stepfamilies Are Not Like Intact Biofamilies! A Summary of 33 Structural Differences": This article compares regular families to stepfamilies and summarizes 33 differences that produce 30 unique *tasks* that stepfamilies must address to succeed.

http://www.stepfamilyinfo.org/compare.htm

Should Same-Sex Marriage Be Permitted?

In 1996 the Circuit Court of Hawaii handed down a landmark decision. In the *Baehr v. Miike* case, the court ruled that Hawaii must issue marriage licenses to gay and lesbian couples, and that denying the right of marriage to lesbians and gays violates the state's constitutional guarantee of equal protection.

In anticipation of the Hawaii decision and the possibility that other states would also have to recognize same-sex marriages, many state legislatures passed laws defining marriage as a union between a man and a woman. In 1996, Congress stepped in and passed, and President Clinton signed, the Defense of Marriage Act, which also defines marriage as an institution available only to heterosexuals.

Some have noted that the increased recognition of domestic partnerships in many jurisdictions makes the movement to legalize same-sex marriage unnecessary. Marriage, however, is an important issue for lesbians and gay men because if domestic partnership is the only vehicle of legal recognition for same-sex relationships, such relationships are relegated to second-class status. Legal recognition of same-sex marriages, they point out, is an important step closer to full equality.

There are many legal rights that lesbians and gays would gain from the right to marry. Joint tax returns, insurance policies, Social Security and pension benefits, property inheritance, and veterans' discounts on medical care, educational loans, and home loans are all examples of the economic benefits that accompany marriage. Next-of-kin status for hospital visits and medical decisions, as well as adoption and guardianship rights, also go along with the right to marry.

Gays and lesbians point out that interracial marriage was once illegal, yet many of the same arguments used to fight the legalization of interracial marriage are used by today's opponents of same-sex marriage.

Those opposed to same-sex marriage argue that the fundamental purpose of marriage is procreation, and that since lesbians and gay men cannot procreate they should not be allowed to marry. Gays and lesbians counter that if we follow this line of reasoning, then infertile heterosexual couples should not be allowed to marry, nor should those straight couples who choose not to have children for any number of reasons.

Andrew Sullivan, in his book *Virtually Normal: An Argument about Homosexuality*, points out that few would deny that many gays and lesbians are capable of the sacrifice, commitment, and responsibilities of marriage. If that is the case and they are denied equal legal standing not because of anything about the relationship itself, but purely because of the involuntary nature of homosexuality itself, then it is a clear example of bias and discrimination.

Same-sex marriage, he points out, would provide role models for gay youth. It would bring the gay couple into the heart of the traditional family and do more to heal the gay-straight rift than any gay rights legislation.

James Q. Wilson, in his response titled "Against Homosexual Marriage," notes that marriage is a sacred union that unites a man and woman for life. It is central to every faith, and every modern society has embraced this view and rejected same-sex marriages. Wilson believes that this view is at the core of what makes society possible.

He wonders why same-sex marriage should be recognized when the high divorce rates show that we are having enough trouble maintaining the institution of marriage at all. If gay and lesbian marriage were legalized, he thinks, such an action would seriously call into question the role of marriage at a time when the threats to it, ranging from single-parent families to divorces, have hit record highs. Support for same-sex marriage would strike most people as a parody of marriage that could further weaken an already strained institution.

Virtually Normal: An Argument about Homosexuality

Andrew
Sullivan

...

Marriage is not simply a private contract; it is a social and public recognition of a private commitment. As such, it is the highest public recognition of personal integrity. Denying it to homosexuals is the most public affront possible to their public equality.

This point may be the hardest for many heterosexuals to accept. Even those tolerant of homosexuals may find this institution so wedded to the notion of heterosexual commitment that to extend it would be to undo its very essence. And there may be religious reasons for resisting this that, within certain traditions, are unanswerable. But I am not here discussing what churches do in their private affairs. I am discussing what the allegedly neutral liberal state should do in public matters. For liberals, the case for homosexual marriage is overwhelming. As a classic public institution, it should be available to any two citizens.

Some might argue that marriage is by definition between a man and a woman; and it is difficult to argue with a definition. But if marriage is articulated beyond this circular fiat, then the argument for its exclusivity to one man and one woman disappears. The center of the public contract is an emotional, financial, and psychological bond between two people; in this respect, heterosexuals and homosexuals are identical. The heterosexuality of marriage is intrinsic only if it is understood to be intrinsically procreative; but that definition has long been abandoned in Western society. No civil marriage license is granted on the condition that the couple bear children; and the marriage is no less legal and no less defensible if it remains childless. In the contemporary West, marriage has become a way in which the state recognizes an emotional commitment by two people to each other for life. And within that definition, there is no public way, if one believes in equal rights under the law, in which it should legally be denied homosexuals.

Of course, no public sanctioning of a contract should be given to people who cannot actually fulfill it. The state rightly, for example, withholds marriage from minors, or from one adult and a minor, since at least one party is unable to understand or live up to the contract. And the state has also rightly barred close family relatives from marriage because familial emotional ties are too strong and powerful to enable a marriage contract to be entered into freely by two autonomous, independent individuals, and because incest poses a uniquely dangerous threat to the trust and responsibility that the family needs to survive. But do homosexuals fall into a similar category? History and experience strongly suggest they don't. Of course, marriage is characterized by a kind of commitment that is rare—and perhaps declining—even among heterosexuals. But it isn't necessary to prove that homosexuals or lesbians are less—or more—able to form long-term relationships than straights for it to be clear that at least *some* are. Moreover, giving these people an equal right to affirm their commitment doesn't reduce the incentive for heterosexuals to do the same.

In some ways, the marriage issue is exactly parallel to the issue of the military. Few people deny that many homosexuals are capable of the sacrifice, the commitment, and the responsibilities of marriage. And indeed, for many homosexuals and lesbians, these responsibilities are already enjoined— as they have been enjoined for centuries. The issue is whether these identical relationships should be denied equal legal standing, not by virtue of anything to do with the relationships themselves but by virtue of the internal, involuntary nature of the homosexuals involved. Clearly, for liberals, the answer to this is clear. Such a denial is a classic case of unequal protection of the laws.

But perhaps surprisingly, … one of the strongest arguments for gay marriage is a conservative one. It's perhaps best illustrated by a comparison with the alternative often offered by liberals and liberationists to legal gay marriage, the concept of "domestic partnership." Several cities in the United States have domestic partnership laws, which allow relationships that do not fit into the category of heterosexual marriage to be registered with the city and qualify for benefits that had previously been reserved for heterosexual married couples. In these cities, a variety of interpersonal arrangements qualify for health insurance, bereavement leave, insurance, annuity and pension rights, housing rights (such as rent-control apartments), adoption, and inheritance rights. Eventually, the aim is to include federal income tax and veterans' benefits as well. Homosexuals are not the only beneficiaries; heterosexual "live-togethers" also qualify.

The conservative's worries start with the ease of the relationship. To be sure, potential domestic partners have to prove financial interdependence, shared living arrangements, and a commitment to mutual caring. But they don't need to have a sexual relationship or even closely mirror old-style marriage. In principle, an elderly woman and her live-in nurse could qualify, or a pair of frat buddies. Left as it is, the concept of domestic partnership could open a Pandora's box of litigation and subjective judicial decision making about who qualifies. You either are or you're not married; it's not a complex question. Whether you are in a domestic partnership is not so clear.

More important for conservatives, the concept of domestic partnership chips away at the prestige of traditional relationships and undermines the priority we give them. Society, after all, has good reasons to extend legal advantages to heterosexuals who choose the formal sanction of marriage over simply living together. They make a deeper commitment to one another and to society; in exchange, society extends certain benefits to them. Marriage provides an anchor, if an arbitrary and often weak one, in the maelstrom of sex and relationships to which we are all prone. It provides a mechanism for emotional stability and economic security. We rig the law in its favor not because we disparage all forms of relationship other than the nuclear family, but because we recognize that not to promote marriage would be to ask too much of human virtue.

For conservatives, these are vital concerns. There are virtually no conservative arguments either for preferring no social incentives for gay relationships or for preferring a second-class relationship, such as domestic partnership, which really does provide an incentive for the decline of traditional marriage. Nor, if conservatives are concerned by the collapse of stable family life, should they be dismayed by the possibility of gay parents. There is no evidence that shows any deleterious impact on a child brought up by two homosexual parents, and considerable evidence that such a parental structure is clearly preferable to single parents (gay or straight) or no effective parents at all, which, alas, is the choice many children now face. Conservatives should not balk at the apparent radicalism of the change involved, either. The introduction of gay marriage would not be some sort of leap in the dark, a massive societal risk. Homosexual marriages have always existed, in a variety of forms; they have just been euphemized. Increasingly they exist in every sense but the legal one. As it has become more acceptable for homosexuals to acknowledge their loves and commitments publicly, more and more have committed themselves to one another for life in full view of their families and friends. A law institutionalizing gay marriage would merely reinforce a healthy trend. Burkean conservatives should warm to the idea.

It would also be an unqualified social good for homosexuals. It provides role models for young gay people, who, after the exhilaration of coming out, can easily lapse into short-term relationships and insecurity with no tangible goal in sight. My own guess is that most homosexuals would embrace such a goal with as much (if not more) commitment as heterosexuals. Even in our society as it is, many lesbian and gay male relationships are virtual textbooks of monogamous commitment; and for many, "in sickness and in health" has become a vocation rather than a vow. Legal gay marriage could also help bridge the gulf often found between homosexuals and their parents. It could bring the essence of gay life—a gay couple—into the heart of the traditional family in a way the family can most understand and the gay offspring can most easily acknowledge. It could do more to heal the gay-straight rift than any amount of gay rights legislation.

More important, perhaps, as gay marriage sank into the subtle background consciousness of a culture its influence would be felt quietly but deeply among gay children. For them, at last, there would be some kind of future; some older faces to apply to their unfolding lives, some language in which their identity could be properly discussed, some rubric by which it could be explained—not in terms of sex, or sexual practices, or bars, or subterranean activity, but in terms of their future life stories, their potential loves, their eventual chance at some kind of constructive happiness. They would be able to feel by the intimation of myriad examples that in this respect their emotional orientation was not merely about pleasure, or sin, or shame, or otherness (although it might always be involved in many of those things), but about the ability to love and be loved as complete, imperfect human beings. Until gay marriage is legalized, this fundamental element of personal dignity will be denied a whole segment of humanity. No other change can achieve it.

Any heterosexual man who takes a few moments to consider what his life would be like if he were never allowed a formal institution to cement his relationships will see the truth of what I am saying. Imagine life without a recognized family; imagine dating without even the possibility of marriage. Any heterosexual woman who can imagine being told at a young age that her attraction to men was wrong, that her loves and crushes were illicit, that her destiny was singlehood and shame, will also appreciate the point. Gay marriage is not a radical step; it is a profoundly humanizing, traditionalizing step. It is the first step in any resolution of the homosexual question—more important than any other institution, since it is the most central institution to the nature of the problem, which is to say, the emotional and sexual bond between one human being and another. If nothing else were done at all, and gay marriage were legalized, 90 percent of the political work necessary to achieve gay and lesbian equality would have been achieved. It is ultimately the only reform that truly matters.

So long as conservatives recognize, as they do, that homosexuals exist and that they have equivalent emotional needs and temptations as heterosexuals, then there is no conservative reason to oppose homosexual marriage and many conservative reasons to support it. So long as liberals recognize, as they do, that citizens deserve equal treatment under the law, then there is no liberal reason to oppose it and many liberal reasons to be in favor of it. So long as intelligent people understand that homosexuals are emotionally and sexually attracted to the same sex as heterosexuals are to the other sex, then there is no human reason on earth why it should be granted to one group and not the other.

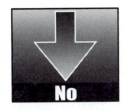

Against Homosexual Marriage

James Q.
Wilson

... [A]n important book has appeared under the title *Virtually Normal*. In it, Andrew Sullivan ... makes a strong case for a new policy toward homosexuals. He argues that "all public (as opposed to private) discrimination against homosexuals be ended.... And that is all." The two key areas where this change is necessary are the military and marriage law. Lifting bans in those areas, while also disallowing antisodomy laws and providing information about homosexuality in publicly supported schools, would put an end to the harm that gays have endured. Beyond these changes, Sullivan writes, American society would need no "cures [of homophobia] or reeducations, no wrenching private litigation, no political imposition of tolerance."

It is hard to imagine how Sullivan's proposals would, in fact, end efforts to change private behavior toward homosexuals, or why the next, inevitable, step would not involve attempts to accomplish just that purpose by using cures and reeducations, private litigation, and the political imposition of tolerance. But apart from this, Sullivan—an English Catholic, a homosexual, and someone who has on occasion referred to himself as a conservative—has given us the most sensible and coherent view of a program to put homosexuals and heterosexuals on the same public footing.

...

When the first books of the Bible were written, and for a long time thereafter, heterosexual love is what seemed at risk. In many cultures—not only in Egypt or among the Canaanite tribes surrounding ancient Israel but later in Greece, Rome, and the Arab world, to say nothing of large parts of

From *Commentary* 101, no. 3 (March 1996). Copyright © 1996. Reprinted with the permission of the author and *Commentary*.

China, Japan, and elsewhere—homosexual practices were common and widely tolerated or even exalted. The Torah reversed this, making the family the central unit of life, the obligation to marry one of the first responsibilities of man, and the linkage of sex to procreation the highest standard by which to judge sexual relations. Leviticus puts the matter sharply and apparently beyond quibble:

> Thou shalt not live with mankind as with womankind; it is an abomination.... If a man also lie with mankind, as he lieth with a woman, both of them have committed an abomination; they shall surely be put to death; their blood shall be upon them.

...

The second argument against homosexual marriage ... is based on natural law as originally set forth by Aristotle and Thomas Aquinas.... How it is phrased varies a bit, but in general its advocates support a position like the following: Man cannot live without the care and support of other people; natural law is the distillation of what thoughtful people have learned about the conditions of that care. The first thing they have learned is the supreme importance of marriage, for without it the newborn infant is unlikely to survive or, if he survives, to prosper. The necessary conditions of a decent family life are the acknowledgment by its members that a man will not sleep with his daughter or a woman with her son and that neither will openly choose sex outside marriage.

Now, some of these conditions are violated, but there is a penalty in each case that is supported by the moral convictions of almost all who witness the violation. On simple utilitarian grounds it may be hard to object to incest or adultery; if both parties to such an act welcome it and if it is secret, what difference does it make? But very few people, and then only ones among the overeducated, seem to care much about mounting a utilitarian assault on the family. To this assault, natural-law theorists respond much as would the average citizen—never mind "utility," what counts is what is right. In particular, homosexual uses of the reproductive organs violate the condition that sex serve solely as the basis of heterosexual marriage.

To Sullivan, what is defective about the natural-law thesis is that it assumes different purposes in heterosexual and homosexual love: moral consummation in the first case and pure utility or pleasure alone in the second. But in fact, Sullivan suggests, homosexual love can be as consummatory as heterosexual. He notes that as the Roman Catholic Church has deepened its understanding of the involuntary—that is, in some sense genetic—basis of homosexuality, it has attempted to keep homosexuals in the church as objects of affection and nurture, while banning homosexual acts as perverse.

But this, though better than nothing, will not work, Sullivan writes. To show why, he adduces an analogy to a sterile person. Such a person is permitted to serve in the military or enter an unproductive marriage; why not homosexuals? If homosexuals marry without procreation, they are no different (he suggests) from a sterile man or woman who marries without hope of procreation. Yet people, I think, want the form observed even when the practice varies; a sterile marriage, whether from choice or necessity, remains a marriage of a man and a woman. To this Sullivan offers essentially an aesthetic response: Just as albinos remind us of the brilliance of color and genius teaches us about moderation, homosexuals are a "natural foil" to the heterosexual union, "a variation that does not eclipse the theme." Moreover, the threat posed by the foil to the theme is slight as compared to the threats posed by adultery, divorce, and prostitution. To be consistent, Sullivan once again reminds us, society would have to ban adulterers from the military as it now bans confessed homosexuals.

But again this misses the point. It would make more sense to ask why an alternative to marriage should be invented and praised when we are having enough trouble maintaining the institution at all. Suppose that gay or lesbian marriage were authorized; rather than producing a "natural foil" that would "not eclipse the theme," I suspect such a move would call even more seriously into question the role of marriage at a time when the threats to it, ranging from single-parent families to common divorces, have hit record highs. Kenneth Minogue recently wrote of Sullivan's book that support for homosexual marriage would strike most people as "mere parody," one that could further weaken an already strained institution.

To me, the chief limitation of Sullivan's view is that it presupposes that marriage would have the same domesticating effect on homosexual members as it has on heterosexuals, while leaving the latter largely unaffected. Those are very large assumptions that no modern society has ever tested.

Nor does it seem plausible to me that a modern society resists homosexual marriages entirely out of irrational prejudice. Marriage is a union, sacred to most, that unites a man and woman together for life. It is a sacrament of the Catholic Church and central to every other faith. Is it out of misinformation that every modern society has embraced this view and rejected the alternative? Societies differ greatly in their attitude toward the income people may have, the relations among their various races, and the distribution of political power. But they differ scarcely at all over the distinctions between heterosexual and homosexual couples. The former are overwhelmingly preferred over the latter. The reason, I believe, is that these distinctions involve the nature of marriage and thus the very meaning—even more, the very possibility—of society.

...

Let us assume for the moment that a chance to live openly and legally with another homosexual is desirable. To believe that, we must set aside biblical injunctions, a difficult matter in a profoundly religious nation. But suppose we manage the diversion, perhaps on the grounds that if most Americans skip church, they can as readily avoid other errors of (possibly) equal magnitude. Then we must ask on what terms the union shall be arranged. There are two alternatives—marriage or domestic partnership.

Sullivan acknowledges the choice, but disparages the domestic-partnership laws that have evolved in some foreign countries and in some American localities. His reasons, essentially conservative ones, are that domestic partnerships are too easily formed and too easily broken. Only real marriages matter. But—aside from the fact that marriage is in serious decline, and that only slightly more than half of all marriages performed in the United States this year will be between never-before-married heterosexuals—what is distinctive about marriage is that it is an institution created to sustain child rearing. Whatever losses it has suffered in this respect, its function remains what it has always been.

The role of raising children is entrusted in principle to married heterosexual couples because after much experimentation—several thousand years, more or less—we have found nothing else that works as well. Neither a gay nor a lesbian couple can of its own resources produce a child; another party must be involved. What do we call this third party? A friend? A sperm or egg bank? An anonymous donor? There is no settled language for even describing, much less approving of, such persons.

Suppose we allowed homosexual couples to raise children who were created out of a prior heterosexual union or adopted from someone else's heterosexual contact. What would we think of this? There is very little research on the matter. Charlotte Patterson's famous essay, "Children of Gay and Lesbian Parents" (*Journal of Child Development* 1992), begins by conceding that the existing studies focus on children born into a heterosexual union that ended in divorce or that was transformed when the mother or father "came out" as a homosexual. Hardly any research has been done on children acquired at the outset by a homosexual couple. We therefore have no way of knowing how they would behave. And even if we had such studies, they might tell us rather little unless they were conducted over a very long period of time.

But it is one thing to be born into an apparently heterosexual family and then many years later to learn that one of your parents is homosexual. It is quite another to be acquired as an infant from an adoption agency or a parent-for-hire and learn from the first years of life that you are, because of your family's position, radically different from almost all other children you will meet. No one can now say how grievous this would be. We know that young children tease one another unmercifully; adding this dimension does not seem to be a step in the right direction.

Of course, homosexual "families," with or without children, might be rather few in number. Just how few, it is hard to say. Perhaps Sullivan himself would marry, but, given the great tendency of homosexual males to be promiscuous, many more like him would not, or if they did, would not marry with as much seriousness.

That is problematic in itself. At one point, Sullivan suggests that most homosexuals would enter a marriage "with as much (if not more) commitment as heterosexuals." Toward the end of his book, however, he seems to withdraw from so optimistic a view. He admits that the label "virtually" in the title of his book is deliberately ambiguous, because homosexuals as a group are not "normal." At another point, he writes that the "openness of the contract" between two homosexual males means that such a union will in fact be more durable than a heterosexual marriage because the contract contains an "understanding of the need for extramarital outlets." But no such "understanding" exists in heterosexual marriage; to suggest that it might in homosexual ones is tantamount to saying that we are now referring to two different kinds of arrangements. To justify this difference, perhaps, Sullivan adds that the very "lack of children" will give "gay couples greater freedom." Freedom for what? Freedom, I think, to do more of those things that heterosexual couples do less of because they might hurt the children.

Key Websites

LSU LAW LIBRARY: GAY MARRIAGE—A SELECTIVE BIBLIOGRAPHY

Although the right to marry is guaranteed to Americans under the Fourteenth Amendment to the U.S. Constitution and cannot be arbitrarily denied, recent events have shown that marriage is actually subject to government control, and this control is now an issue of public debate. This selective bibliography is intended to serve as a starting point for those individuals interested in researching the topic of gay marriage.
http://www.law.lsu.edu/library/biblio/samesex.htm

SAME-SEX MARRIAGE RESOURCES

This site is in favor of same-sex marriage, and provides links to Web pages, online articles, books, general discussion sites, and law journals.
http://www.calico-company.com/formboston/links.htm

PARTNERS TASK FORCE FOR GAY & LESBIAN COUPLES

This site provides extensive information on issues of concern to same-sex couples, including legal marriage and sources of support. It presents the results of their national couples survey on attitudes toward legal marriage for same-sex couples. It contains legal information, essays, research, ceremonies, and links to organizations and groups involved in same-sex marriage.
http://www.buddybuddy.com/toc.html

HUMAN RIGHTS CAMPAIGN

This site contains some of the information and resources that the staff of this group working for gay and lesbian rights uses to inform members of Congress and the public about issues of importance to the lesbian, gay, bisexual, and transgendered communities. One section of this site contains specific laws and acts relating to same-sex marriage.
http://www.hrc.org/issues/marriage/index.html

EXECUTIVE SUMMARY OF THE REPORT OF THE CITY UNIVERSITY OF NEW YORK STUDY GROUP ON DOMESTIC PARTNERSHIPS

The CUNY Study Group on Domestic Partnerships examined the issue of providing University benefits to the domestic partners of lesbian and gay CUNY employees. The report presents the group's findings on current practices and

procedures of various municipalities, universities, and private industry firms. It also presents the pertinent literature in this emerging area of employee relations.
http://www.cs.cmu.edu/afs/cs.cmu.edu/user/scotts/domestic-partners/cuny.html

RECOGNITION OF SAME-SEX MARRIAGE: TIME FOR CHANGE?

Inge Lauw, *Recognition of Same-Sex Marriage: Time for Change?*: A research article that discusses the cases relating to legal recognition of same-sex marriages. The article also examines policy arguments for and against granting marriage licenses to same-sex couples. It contains an extensive list of references.
http://www.murdoch.edu.au/elaw/issues/v1n3/lauw2.txt

LESBIAN AND GAY MARRIAGE THROUGH HISTORY AND CULTURE

Paul Halsall, *Lesbian and Gay Marriage through History and Culture*: This paper seeks to establish that same-sex marriages did occur in sufficiently diverse historical and cultural contexts as to refute the assertion that "marriage" is irretrievably or "naturally" heterosexual.
http://www.bway.net/~halsall/lgbh/lgbh-marriage.html